50 Ideas
to Train Your Sales Staff
in 15 Minutes a Day

50 IDEAS
TO TRAIN YOUR SALES STAFF IN
15 MINUTES
A DAY
FOR RETAIL MUSIC BUSINESSES

BOB POPYK

HAL LEONARD BOOKS
AN IMPRINT OF HAL LEONARD CORPORATION

Published in 2013 by Hal Leonard Books
An Imprint of Hal Leonard Corporation
7777 West Bluemound Road
Milwaukee, WI 53213

Trade Book Division Editorial Offices
33 Plymouth St., Montclair, NJ 07042

Printed in the United States of America

Book design by Mark Lerner

Library of Congress Cataloging-in-Publication Data

Popyk, Bob.
 50 ideas to train your sales staff in 15 minutes a day : for retail music businesses / Bob Popyk.
    p. cm.
 Includes bibliographical references.
 1. Selling. 2. Sales management. 3. Marketing. 4. Music stores--Management. I. Title. II. Title: Fifty ideas to train your sales staff in 15 minutes a day.
 HF5438.25.P665 2012
 658.3'1245--dc23
                        2012039990

ISBN 978-1-4584-2528-7

www.halleonardbooks.com

Contents

Preface

This book is intended for independent music retailers with both a full-time and part-time sales staff. Its sole purpose is to help dealers train their sales staff to create more customers and more business with ideas that can be used quickly and easily.

It seems as though sales training is limited or almost nonexistent today in many independent music stores. A number of stores do not have regular sales meetings, if any at all. Salespeople come and go. A little training, even for just a few minutes a day, can work wonders.

While not every idea described in this book is for everyone, there are many things that could easily work for you. This book lists 50 ideas to incorporate into 10- to 15-minute daily meetings. There are ideas that you can give your sales staff to use as soon as your doors open. Remember: play to your strengths, pick and choose what is right for you, and put your mind to it if you want to see some positive results. Start by taking the ideas you like best and giving them a try. You will be amazed how much business can be gained with just a little knowledge passed along on a daily basis. You never know what works until you give it a try.

Acknowledgments

Thanks to all of the readers of my column in *The Music Trades* magazine, and to the National Association of Music Merchants (NAMM), who have helped keep me in touch with the indie music dealers all over the country.

Also, a sincere thank-you goes to the staff of Bentley-Hall Inc., who have worked with me over so many years. They made my job much easier, and now I feel as though I never had to work a day in my life.

After all of the years as an owner of several music stores, and then as a writer on sales and marketing strategies, I really believe that the retail music business is a fun business. And the more money you make, the more fun you're going to have.

I hope this book helps maximize the fun of being a music dealer.

Bob Popyk
RPopyk@aol.com

50 Ideas
to Train Your Sales Staff
in 15 Minutes a Day

1

Getting Started

Sales training is not an easy subject for music retailers. First of all, who has the time? Secondly, what if you train your staff and then they quit? As a matter of fact, what if you *don't* train them and they stick around? Well, here's another take on it: if you don't train your staff to sell, you are going to see money walking out the door.

While marketing is one way to drive sales and lure new customers into your store, advertising and promotion are expensive, particularly using major media. It takes a big checkbook (not to mention an even bigger crystal ball) to know where to spend your money. Getting salespeople personally involved in finding their own customers, and selling to them once they come into the store, will be the answer in the years to come. Just the basics of selling, regularly put to use, will generate more sales week after week, month after month. It's not that hard, but you have to really want it. It becomes much easier if you have the right game plan, the right attitude, and the willingness to give new ideas a try.

Having an untrained sales staff is like having a vending machine on your sales floor. When you have clerks who simply take money and give back product (like the machines), your sales will suffer.

Sharing some sales smarts with your staff in order to maximize every customer interaction can add tremendously to your bottom line, and to do it, you don't need to spend hours at a time in training. You don't need to have volumes of material with charts and graphs. You can easily do it before you open at a time when everyone is around, in about 10 to 15 minutes each day. If you spend those 10 to 15 minutes a day on just one subject, that could add up to over an hour a week on six different subjects! It's hardly a humungous chunk of time taken from your day, and these few short sessions could add more sales instantly.

You may be asking yourself, "Why should I? It's not my employees and their sales methods that are not working; it's the economy and the spending nature of the public." Whether or not this statement is true is a whole different subject, but it all comes down to this: whether business is slow and you are heading for disaster or whether your business is just fine and always has been, change will never occur without action. If things are not going to your liking, then you have to do something about it or just give up. The next time you think business is slow, forget moaning and complaining. That is just negative energy. Think instead about what you might be able to do to get business where you want it.

Increasing sales is something you can start right now. All you need is a plan and an open mind. Keep these facts in mind as you read through these ideas to ramp up your team's sales skills.

Have a Plan

Your sales staff relies on you to keep work flow grounded and structured. If you are going to have a daily meeting, be prepared for what you are going to discuss, and get right to business. Here is an idea: Take an afternoon to yourself without a computer, cell phone, iPad, or any other distraction. Or enjoy an evening with just you plus a legal pad and pen. Jot down some sales goals, and then write down as many ideas as you can on how you will find more people to talk to and make more sales once customers come into the store. Then come up with a structure on how to get your employees to help you reach them. While sales training can be enjoyable, it is still business. Your employees will take things more seriously if you do.

Get Everyone on Board

It only takes one employee rolling his or her eyes or yawning during a training session to get everyone else antsy and starting to question your purpose. Be persistent and encouraging. Remind your employees that training is beneficial to increasing sales and in turn increasing their own personal paychecks. Be mindful of who is bringing down the morale of your group, and find a way to decrease this negativity.

Be Open-Minded

You have a plan, you have a goal, and you have carefully calculated steps to achieving the revenue of your dreams. While this structure and discipline are important to achieving the outcomes you hope for, do not dismiss ideas that your employees suggest along the way. You never know where the next creative sales idea is going to come from. Not only could their ideas be genius to your plan, they will also contribute to keeping your group involved in the training process and just as enthusiastic as you are.

Stress a Thoughtful Attitude

Personality skills, creativeness, cleverness, and tact do pay off when you are trying to put a sales strategy together. They are also essential for repeat business. This book lists scenarios that will most likely occur over and over again while working in retail. It is important that you are aware of which scenario you are in at a particular time and the appropriate ways to sway the outcome in your favor. Also, it is more important to think about what it might take to get the customer to like *you* than your instrument or product. And a little tact along the way could be the answer.

2

Greet Everyone Who Comes In

What a concept. Talk to people. Say hello to everyone who walks through your door. While this is an obvious concept, you would not believe how many music stores have salespeople who let customers roam around without being approached, greeted, or talked to in any way. They stay behind the counter and play on their computers or cell phones. If you ignore the people who walk in, the next thing you know, they are walking out. They are not an intrusion on your day. Greet them. Make them feel welcome.

During the first 10 seconds after a customer walks through the door, he or she should be recognized. It is pretty simple. Employees should say something like:

(1) "Good morning/afternoon."
(2) "Welcome!"
(3) "Hello."

Pretty simple, huh? While it is not rocket science, it does incorporate some psychology. Try not to say anything that can be answered with a yes or no. Avoid saying, "Can I help you?" Acknowledging customers upon their arrival increases the importance of their visit and demonstrates your excitement about having them there, which in turn may trigger their own excitement about being there. A feeling of importance helps boost self-esteem, the customers' sense of awareness for their personal needs, and perhaps a complete disregard for any budget constraints.

Next, the salesperson should approach the customer and ask questions like:

(1) "What brings you in today?"
(2) "Are you a musician?"

Remember: forget saying, "Can I help you?" Most of the time you'll get a useless response. Let's be honest, what type of answers do you expect from customers? Unless the customer is really looking to buy or desperately wants information, "Can I help you?" will mostly likely result in a "No, thank you."

In any sales situation, you will get a greater response if you first give the customer a reason why he or she should answer you. In doing so, you will close more deals and increase instrument sales. So how do you do that? The key elements of your new introduction are:

(1) Your name.
(2) Your position, skill, qualification, or experience.
(3) How you can help the customer.
(4) An open question to start the conversation. That is, a question that begins with who, what, where, when, or why, and does not result in a yes or no response.

Think about it. How many times have you gone into a store as a customer and nobody talked to you? Some salespeople/clerks just don't want to bother. They let customers look, and if they want to buy something, they have to bring it to the counter or find a salesperson to interrupt—acts that most people just do not have the time and energy for. It happens every day. Simple sales strategy starts with opening your mouth and talking to the customer.

So, you've acknowledged the customer, made him or her feel recognized, and built a foundation for a sales relationship between you and him or her. Now it is time to get a feel for his or her intentions, personality, and current mood, in order to quickly and effectively formulate a plan of action. Remember, every customer is different. What worked on your last customer might not work on this one. You cannot rely on the same set of sales methods over and over again. Many customers *know* your sales intent and will do what they can to deter you. Surprise them.

3

Conversation 101: The Basics

Within the first 30 seconds after greeting customers, you should start a dialogue. Here is the way it works: you talk, they talk, and you talk again. It is called *conversation*. Find out what type of music they like, what instruments they play, and what instruments are currently in their homes. Find out who else plays in their families. The ideas are endless. Getting customers to talk gets them to like you. If they feel you are their friend, they are more apt to buy from you.

Here are two basic methods to keep in mind when striking up a conversation with a customer.

Number 1: Get Personal

Does your personality come through when you talk to a customer? People will speak with, and respect, those they consider a peer. The more comfortable you sound, the easier it will be to put a sale together. We tune out, and are often annoyed by, unemotional sales pitches. Pitches like the ones you hear when you pick up the phone—after saying hello several times—and a monotone voice greets you with,

"Hello, can I speak to [insert bad pronunciation of your name]?" Then the script reading begins.

Of course you want to be prepared when you describe your instruments and accessories. The worst time to be thinking about what you will say is when it is about to leave your mouth. For example, think about the bad acting you've seen in plays or movies. It probably sounded stilted and unnatural—like it was being read. When you talk to a customer, you want to come across as a friend, not a machine—a fellow musician, not an idiot.

If customers want to deal with a cold, impersonal source, they will go to the Internet or a catalogue. You are at an advantage because you can use personality, inflection, kindness, understanding, and warmth when you meet a customer. You can make customers friends, get them to smile, and have them refer you to their friends and families. Take advantage of it.

If you have to, tweak your personality. Find out what kinds of music your customers like to play or listen to. Get them to laugh a little. The music business is a fun business. The more instruments you sell, the more fun it can be. Let your human touch show through.

Number 2: Speak the Customers' Language

All things being equal, customers like to do business with someone they can relate to. If your prices and services are pretty much the same as your competitor's, customers are likely to choose to do business with someone they *like*. They buy on emotion and shy away from salespeople who annoy or irritate them. It is common sense.

So, how can you relate better to your customers? Speaking and understanding your customers' language is a good place to start. You don't have to be bilingual. It means being able to understand and converse in whatever your customers' musical tastes and cultural dialects are, whether it is jive, hip hop, adult, cool, senior citizen, urban, suburban, country, or hundreds of others.

People like people who are like themselves. In other words, if people can relate to you, they will like you. If they like you, they will trust you. If they trust you, they are more apt to buy from you.

If your store is in an ethnic section of your city, or if you have a lot of customers who speak other languages, learning a few of their native words shows that you are trying to be one of them. You don't have to speak fluently. They speak English. Try to understand a few words of their language.

If you are a younger salesperson talking to an older person (that is, anyone 10 years older than you), you might want to put yourself in their shoes. Talk in terms they can understand. Don't use the latest slang or overly technical terms. Also, they probably would not appreciate being called "dude," or even "ma'am."

Someone from New York City may have a presence, an attitude, a speech pattern that is all his or her own. You have to figure it out for yourself. This goes for customers from Los Angeles, Minneapolis, Dallas, or any other region. You have to adapt to their styles. It's called *mirroring*.

We have all had customers who want to beat us up verbally so they can buy something for less than its value, then tell us they will be back, only to end up buying down the street. Maybe we just haven't spoken their language. Maybe it is not the price, the service, or the product. Maybe it is *you*.

Speaking your customers' language does not mean taking a three-day Berlitz course. It means talking to them in terms they can understand, words they recognize, and phrases they can relate to. If you know all of the industry jargon and your customer is an uneducated novice, it is like speaking Portuguese to a Ukrainian.

Do not talk over your customers' heads. Do not be too cool, too clever, or too technical. Know where the fine line is. Talk to your customers in a language they will understand, but first find out what their language actually is. Everything else will be easy.

4

Conversation 102:
After You Greet Your Customer

Once you have established grounds for a conversation with a customer, it is time to get down to business. Let's find out with whom you are talking. Introduce yourself and ask your customer's name. It is easy. Introduce yourself first. It is uncomfortable to have someone know who you are and not know who he or she is. Giving your customer your name is a great way to begin building a relationship.

An easy way to stroke people's egos and make them feel important is to use their names when you speak to them. Here are a few methods that will make using your customer's name work especially well.

Be respectful. Using customers' last names (Mr. Smith, Ms. Johnson, Ms. Jones) is probably your best bet until you have developed a close relationship (unless they have introduced themselves by their first name only).

Say their names correctly. If you are not sure, ask them; don't guess. Most people are picky about having their names spelled and pronounced correctly. Be sincere. If you are just rattling the customer's name off as part of your canned pitch, or if you only look at customers' credit cards for their names and never make smiling eye contact, you are probably eroding the relationship, not building it.

Be sensitive. Always be aware of how your customers want to be treated. If they are casual, chatty, and friendly, using their names will probably be a plus. If they are formal, stilted, or rushed, they may feel you are taking liberties by using their names.

Get right to the point. Simple speaking can have great rewards. When it becomes long, complicated, and overdone, it can have the opposite effect.

Be competitive and get right to the point. Do it in words that everyone can understand. If you have to, use only one- and two-syllable words. Being clever at the same time is not a bad idea either. Ever notice that when you thumb through a magazine quickly and spot a cartoon on a certain page, you always go back and read it? You know that it is quick, easy to read, and might make you smile. You might skip the lengthy stories and articles, but you always glance at the cartoons.

In selling, if you start rambling without getting a customer's attention first, people start looking for other things to focus on. Getting to the point *quickly* can make the difference.

Try this: Somewhere in your store (on an item you would like customers to ask about), place a small sign that says "Don't Ask." See how many people ask about it. Human nature is something else. If you took the same item and listed 15 features and benefits—along with price, discount, and savings—you would not get half the amount of interest in the item.

One of the biggest mistakes salespeople make is overselling the product. That goes for the company whose advertising and marketing strategies sometimes go off on tangents as well. For the salesperson, just find a need and fill it. For advertising, show how a need can be filled. And be quick about it. It can be that simple.

Getting right to the point can free up a lot of time for you when talking to a customer. When you get the first sign of positive acceptance, ask, "Would you like to get it?" If the customer says yes, you could easily save yourself an hour of sales babble.

We live in an age of complicated communication, overwrought with high technology and bombarded with thousands of sales and marketing messages. Make it easy for your prospect. Just get right to the point.

5

Avoiding "Nerve Words"

Remember George Carlin's "Seven Words You Can Never Say on Television"? Well, in selling musical instruments, those seven words are only a start. If you have been selling for any length of time, you know that there are a lot of words, phrases, topics, and discussions you cannot get into unless you want to run the risk of really irritating someone . . . to the point where he or she will not buy from you regardless of price. If you are new to selling, here is an idea of where you do not want to go.

There are some guidelines you should be aware of. If you are the type of salesperson who likes to "shoot from the hip," there are some things you should avoid:

(1) Four-letter words that you cannot use on the airwaves.
(2) Sexual innuendoes.
(3) Discussions relating to sex or sexual preferences.
(4) Religious convictions.
(5) Political views.
(6) Discussion of ethnic backgrounds.
(7) Opinions on multilevel marketing programs.

(8) Self-praise.
(9) Making fun of someone's musical taste.
(10) Anything controversial.

If a customer starts using expletives in the course of conversation, should you try to be his buddy and start using them back? Probably not. Better you bring the customer up to your level, rather than let him drag you down to his. Remember the saying "Familiarity breeds contempt"? Think about it next time you want to join in with your best Andrew Dice Clay or Lisa Lampanelli dialogue. Save it for the local bar.

Don't even think about commenting on anything to do with marriage, sex, or alternative lifestyles. If a man says, "I would like to buy this guitar, but I need to discuss it with my wife first," do not come back with, "What kind of wimp are you?" This kind of response won't sell many instruments. Friendliness, compassion, and common sense probably will.

If, while creating rapport with your customer, the subject of religion, politics, or sex comes up, change the subject quickly. You don't know where your customer stands. A middle-of-the-road policy is easy to tap dance to.

Think that everyone shares your musical tastes? Try making light of accordions or ethnic music. Most people make a little fun of polkas once in a while. Miller beer tried it with a commercial in a hip and trendy bar, where a customer says he is going to put money in the jukebox to play a polka, and the whole bar goes quiet. Funny, huh? The thousands of letters and complaints Miller received from polka lovers made them think otherwise. They pulled it after the first run.

Something else. Pull back on self-praise. The "We're the biggest, the best, the greatest" approach worked for Muhammad Ali. It may cost you sales if you overdo it. Humbling yourself with phrases like "I want to earn your business" or "I want to make sure that you are satisfied" can run rings around your competition.

The point is this: Be very aware of your customers' feelings and sensitive to their likes and dislikes. Don't stereotype people into categories. Be nice. Watch your mouth. Try a few random acts of kindness. Get to know your customers better, but stay away from all of the topics listed previously. Find out where they live, their work and their hobbies. Talk about books, movies, sports, or musical instruments they have owned in the past. Avoid the danger areas. You want to make a sale and a friend. When something controversial comes up, do a little sidestep. Once you tick people off, it can be very hard to get them to buy from you, and almost impossible to get them into the store to see you again.

6

Selling Creatively Using Common Sense

To be good at selling musical instruments, you need some basic skills, some street smarts, a little persistence, a fair amount of personality, and some common sense. You don't need 55 closes, a degree in psychology, or three different selling systems under your belt. But you do have to *ask* people to buy.

Think about it. In the auto business, many successful car salespeople openly admit that they do not have the slightest idea what they are doing. They tell customers that right up front. How many times have you heard them ask, "What do I have to do to sell you this car?" They must put those deals together somehow.

On the other end of the spectrum, some of the best salespeople are at McDonald's. You place an order, and you hear, "Would you like fries with that?" It's called *suggestive selling*. Asking for the order. It works.

If you ever go to Nordstrom, the department store giant, take a trip to the shoe department and ask to try on a pair of shoes. The salespeople never bring out one pair. They bring out three. One is the pair that you wanted to try, another is the same style but a different color, and the third is a completely different shoe that they thought you might like. Then they might ask you if you want to buy all three.

Try to read your customer's mind. It would be great if we had the power to know what goes on inside our customers' heads when we show them a new guitar, set of drums, or state-of-the-art digital piano. When you ask them if they would like to buy it, do they say, "I want to think it over"? What are they really thinking? Does that "think it over" really mean, "I want to check the Internet"?

Okay, maybe we don't have the power to read minds, and maybe we can't predict the future, but we can anticipate what the outcome will be. We can ask customers questions where we already know in advance what the answers will be. We can lead them where we want them to go. This can take our sales skills up a notch or two right away.

You could call this anticipatory closing, predictable qualifying, or any number of fancy terms. Actually, it is more like "common-sense selling." If you already know the answers to questions you are going to ask, you are more likely to make more sales. You anticipate a positive response. "No, I don't want it" is not an option.

If you are selling a piano and the issue is price, what if you asked, "How would you like a bench that holds music?" Most people would. Most benches have a lift-top lid. You anticipate a yes, and the more positive responses you get out of a customer, the closer you are to a sale.

If you are selling a guitar, and you ask, "Are you going to want extra strings?" and then ask how many sets the customer would like, you are way past the point of asking for the guitar sale. You anticipated the sale. Now it is just the matter of add-ons.

If you are selling an electronic keyboard for the home and during the demo you ask, "Would you play this if you had it in your home?" you know what the answer will be. Anticipatory selling. It can work.

When a customer comes in to buy an accessory item and asks if you have a certain type of drumstick, a particular set of strings, or a certain model of microphone, instead of merely saying yes, try saying, "Certainly, how many would you like?" Anticipate that he or she will want more than one. And while the customer is thinking about your question, you can suggest a quantity. Anticipate that customers will need more than they came in for, and you might just get what you anticipated.

How about this: When customers come looking for an expensive instrument and tell you in advance that this is the first place they have looked, anticipate that this is going to be their major objection for not buying then and there. Anticipate their objection, and head it off at the pass. You can say things like, "Obviously you are a pro at this. I bet you are wondering why these are so cheap." Or throw in, "We don't have many of these, so you might want to make a quick decision before they are gone." If it applies, you could say, "Would you like to use this for your gig tonight? I can make it happen for you." Anticipate that they are revved up about the ax, and want to use it right away, and don't want to look like a weenie in your eyes. You sell to the best musicians, don't you? Make your prospects want to be included in that group. Anticipate what questions will play to their egos.

Sometimes, you want to anticipate that you're going to get beaten up over price. Don't let customer knowledge of discount prices from other dealers take you by surprise. Anticipate that customers have this in their brains before they open their mouths. Sell yourself, your store, and the instrument all at the same time. And when you say, "Hey, didn't you open for Toby Keith?" and you know the answer is no, anticipate that at least you have their attention and they will know you think that they are one of the best players who ever came into the store. They are. They are your customers. Play to your audience.

7

Handling Objections 101: Get Your Customer to Talk a Little More

What are some of the objections you hear every day from someone not buying a specific instrument? Perhaps these examples sound familiar:

(1) "I am waiting for my tax refund check."
(2) "It's a little out of my budget range."
(3) "I need to check with my spouse."
(4) "I want to look around."
(5) "I want to check the classifieds."
(6) "I am going to check the Internet first."
(7) "I have only just started to look around."
(8) "I want to think about it."
(9) "I don't have the money or credit right now."

There are ways to handle these objections in one word or less. Actually it is pretty easy. Get your customers to keep talking. You could say something like:

(1) "Why?"
(2) "And?"

(3) "What do you mean by that?"

(4) Or just say nothing.

For example, if your customer says that he has just started to shop for an instrument, you could ask him to clarify ("What does that mean?"). Your customer will talk a little more and may even tell you a different story as to why he is not buying right away.

You could also repeat the statement as a question. If a customer says that she would like to look around, ask her, "You want to look around?" Then see what she says. You may be surprised by what comes out of her mouth.

Here is the whole key to answering objections: you need to get your customers to talk, and you need to get them to like you. It does not matter what the objection is; you can simply ask why and let the customer talk some more. Many times they will talk themselves right into buying the instrument.

8

Handling Objections 102: Don't Confuse Your Customer

It is a good idea to determine your customers' *information threshold* right from the start. How much do they really want to know? How much information do they have already? How much do you really have to tell them in order to get them to buy an instrument? How much before they start going in the opposite direction?

Every store's products and services are different. Yet one common denominator between customers is that if you confuse them or tell them too much information, they might just keep shopping . . . elsewhere. When the next customer says, "I'll think about it," maybe he is really saying, "I have *too much* to think about."

Customers can only take in so much technical information before their brains start to overload. There are computers, refrigerators, microwaves, digital keyboards, digital cameras, digital answering machines, stereos, VCRs, and DVRs (not to mention the owners' manuals that look like pages from a bar exam). It seems as though nothing is simple anymore. Yet, it is not how much technical data we have stored in our brains that is starting to be a problem. The problem is how much time we spend studying, reading, watching, listening, and learning about new technology that takes hours out of our days and years out of our lives (while draining our wallets).

The simpler you make it for the customer to understand your product, the easier it is to sell. The problem many times is that the salespeople know so much about their products (oftentimes taking months to figure out) and they expect to cram it into the brains of the customers in three minutes or less. It does not work that way. Customers are starting to go for easier and simpler, rather than complicated.

Here is where you can make things easier for your customers. You might tell them you are very familiar with the instrument and suggest that it would be perfect for them. Maybe you own one yourself. Maybe someone else the customer might be familiar with owns one.

Remember, at the first sign of positive acceptance, ask customers if they would like to get the product. Many times they simply say yes. You never know. Let the customer talk. You don't want to keep going and going without getting any kind of feedback. In fact, you want to be careful of going way past the point where your customer has already decided to buy. The same way customers may talk themselves into a sale, sometimes you might just talk yourself right out of one.

9

Handling Objections 103: You Don't Know Jack

Jack is an above-middle-aged man with a few bucks in his pocket who frequently visits your store. He tends to be a little selective when spending those bucks, but the fact of the matter is: he does spend them. He has lots of toys and nice things. But Jack will not buy a product that he cannot fully understand while it is being explained to him in a store. He doesn't like to waste time reading directions. He has never read the owner's manual to his car. He can't (or doesn't want to) program his DVR. He will not do business with a company that has an automated answering system where he can't press 0 and get a live person. He will not buy a product from a salesperson who talks in technical babble, or from anyone who treats him like a secondary citizen, a dummy, or an intrusion on his or her day. His favorite expression to salespeople is, "I may be crazy, but I'm not stupid." That is, he doesn't want to appear stupid.

Guess what. There are a lot of Jacks (and Jackies) running around out there. And the sooner you get to know them, the more sales you will make. Granted, not everybody is like Jack, and the ones who are won't have labels on their foreheads reading, "Make it simple and I will buy!" Not everyone is alike. Some people enjoy techno-spar, and that is just fine. You can probably hold your own with the best of them. Product knowledge, features, and inner components are probably your strong points.

But one- and two-syllable words are Jack's strong points. People like him love hearing words like *easy* and *simple*. They like phrases like "nothing to it" and "plug in and use." These are the people who revel in "no assembly required." They love "easy to buy" and "easy to use." They don't want a customer service number to call; they want to be able to call you. They know that customer service representatives put them on hold for days, don't give them the information they want, disconnect them, and are less than friendly. If you do an end-run around all of these built-up objections, problems, and concerns, you will probably sell to Jack in no time flat. And you won't have to discount either. Jack will be so happy he will refer you to all of his other Jack-friends, and may even invite you to dinner.

The next time a Jack comes into your store, get to know him a little bit first. Find out where his technical information limit is. Does he have a VCR, a 35 mm camera, and audiocassettes rather than CDs, a digital camera, or an MP3 player? For the people who like things simple, hide the owner's manual and save the techno-talk. Your product may have bells and whistles that Jack may become comfortable with once it is in his home, but right now, what is the main benefit? What is the one reason he is going to love it and should buy it right now? Don't ever talk over his head. Be his friend. Appreciate the fact that his computer on-off switch was hard to find, that he threw his palm pilot away in favor of his paper calendar and still longs for the days of rotary-dial phones with flashing hold buttons. Support him. Agree with him. And tell him how much to write the check out for as your instrument goes out with him.

You just have to know Jack.

10

How to Handle Customers You Just Can't Stand

Do you ever have customers come into your store who just drive you nuts? Possibly many of these people return again and again. Maybe it is their looks, their attitudes, their personalities, or their breath. How do you handle it?

If you are in the music business, dealing with "different" people is a fact of life. It comes with the territory. You have got to be able to shift gears if you are going to make sales. And it is more than knowing how to do it. Wanting to do it is equally important. Whether you believe it or not, there is more to selling than knowing your instruments, qualifying your customers, and asking for the sale.

Maybe you have never had a customer who makes your blood pressure rise, or who rattles your cage until you start to spit. Maybe you are selling to every single person who comes into your store, and maybe you can handle every off-the-wall situation, but in the event that you occasionally have someone who plucks your nerves, here are a few suggestions.

First of all, if you find yourself face to face with someone you would like to tell to shove off, remember that customers are critical to the profitability of your business. They have friends who could also end up being your customers, and you don't need a string of people bad-mouthing you and your store. Keep in mind that not all people are alike, and because of different personalities and temperaments, occasionally you're going to run into people who rub you the wrong way. The easiest way to get someone to like you is to find something about him or her that you truly like. Sometimes you have to really search.

Then keep in mind that the Golden Rule has to be modified if you really want to crank your sales up a notch. The Golden Rule (in case it wasn't a part of your upbringing) is: *Do unto others as you would have them do unto you.* The platinum version of the Golden Rule is: *Do unto others as they would want to be done unto.* You will find that many customers do not care about you. They care about themselves. If you don't like them, too bad.

Something else: people like people who are like themselves. If you try to sell to everyone without consciously modifying your primary personality style, you will get in the way of the sale 75 percent of the time. If you don't change your approach, you might find another sale going down the drain (or worse, to your competition). Also, keep this in mind: customers like salespeople who are good conversationalists . . . and good conversationalists are those who can get other people to talk about themselves.

11

Dealing with Customers You *Really* Can't Stand

How about the customer who comes in with a chip on his shoulder? Maybe he wants to put you up on the auction block when you tell him how much a certain instrument costs. Or maybe he wants you to know how "nearly famous" he is, and wants you to kiss his feet because you are so privileged that he is coming through your door. How about the customer who wants your best price because she is going to shop all of your competitors, all of the catalogs, and all of the Internet to find it cheaper somewhere else? Ever have any of these?

You have two options:

(1) Give them a whack right on the sides of their heads and send them out of the door.
(2) Try to identify your customers' primary personality styles, and then suppress the aspects of yours that they are most likely to find objectionable. Then try to figure out how to get them to like you. Emphasize the aspects of your personality that are most likely to be compatible with the customers.

Again, if people like you, they are more apt to trust you. If they trust you, they are more apt to buy from you.

It is a great feeling to be able to say, "Look pal, you can take your crummy attitude and your nickel-and-dime, penny-pinching, better-than-thou attitude, and hit the road." But instead, you could choose to sell to everyone and create a base of business that will pay dividends for years to come.

As for Mr. Know-It-All . . .

We have all had them. They come in many forms. Both male and female, young and old. They not only know it all, their parents knew it all. They've had uncles and cousins who have known it all. Don't try to explain a new instrument to them. They have been there, done that. Don't tell them what a value that new guitar or drum set is. They know the manufacturer personally. They may have been consulted before it went to market. They can buy it direct at cost (even less from a catalog). And they have heard there is this site on the Internet that is practically giving them away. They have played professionally, played as a child, have friends who are musicians, or have a relative who gave them all the advice they need to buy an instrument.

Maybe the customer is a parent renting a horn for his child. He used to play the same horn during the War. Would have played professionally except for getting shot by a wayward bullet when playing taps one day. Could have played with Miller, Dorsey, Monk, and Miles. Knew them all. Don't tell him about horns. ("What is that spit valve thing for, by the way?")

Then you've got the pro, or semipro (make that wannabe-pro). Digital keyboards? Heck, not only does he know them backwards and forwards, he builds them, fixes them, and programs them on his breaks during the morning shift at McDonald's. If he can get it way-less-than-wholesale, he will send you plenty of customers when he is seen playing it out at weekend weddings and those free audition nights at the local bar.

How do you handle these people? First of all, do you even want to handle these people? Let's just assume for a moment that sales are really important to you and you want to sell to these people in spite of themselves. That will show them. Teach them a thing or two with your instrument going out of the door with their money in your pocket.

But how do you do it? How do you handle the know-it-alls before they just tick you off completely? First of all, Mr. Know-It-All likes to hear some particular words and phrases.

(1) "Wow, I'm impressed!"
(2) "I would love to get your opinion on this."
(3) "What would you do if you were me?"
(4) "Could I use you as a referral if you buy it from our store?"
(5) "You sure play great, you must have been playing for years."
(6) "Man, I wish I could do that."
(7) "That guitar looks like it was made for you."
(8) "Can I get your advice?"
(9) "I'm sure any store in town would love to get your business."
(10) "I want to earn your business."

You get the picture. Unfortunately, we have to be nice. That is really hard when you want to give someone a slap on the side of the head. But don't lose your cool.

12

How About Customers Who Just Can't Stand *You*?

Not everyone is going to like you. So find out what you and your customers have in common. Emulate your customers. Get them to laugh. Be their friend; don't run down their attitude, their choice in music, the competition, or their talent.

Do not use phrases like:

(1) "Then go somewhere else."
(2) "That store will be broke in a month."
(3) "Here, let *me* show you how good it sounds."
(4) "If you buy it somewhere else, don't look to us for service in the future."
(5) "You've never taken lessons, right?"
(6) "I will give you one price, and if you want it, fine. I am not going to haggle with you all day."

Remember, nasty people don't like pressure. They can't stand it. You must realize, in spite of everything you might think, "nasties" are musicians, and musicians do buy instruments somewhere. They will pay more than wholesale when they think that value exceeds price and the salesperson is their friend. It is a fact. It is usually just one of those two things that is a problem when Mr. Pain-in-the-Butt walks out of your store and buys down the street.

Dealing with Mr. and Ms. Nasty can be very trying. It can be tough. But if they are looking for an instrument, they are going to buy it somewhere. If you have the tolerance, the tenacity, the personality, and the power to hang in there while they do a number on your head, you might luck out. Your competition will probably send them packing, thinking they've just scored a victory by not having to deal with them. If you shift gears, tell them what they want to hear, and make them your friends, they might just end up as regular customers. It is up to you.

Think about this: How do *you* handle nasty customers? How do *you* handle the person who complains and gives you a rough time?

There are plenty of ways of handling a customer who thinks he or she can get it cheaper somewhere else. Three rounds of verbal sparring is not the answer. In the case of the customer who has an unreasonable demand or an unwarranted complaint, ignoring her only compounds the problem. Trying to see her side, while stating your position politely and reasonably, will let your customer keep her dignity. It could also result in future business with your store if you handle the customer the right way.

Remember, music is supposed to add happiness to a person's life. A case of the nasties only gets in the way. Customer nastiness is a disease that can be cured! And you, the seller, have the remedy.

13

Six Misconceptions When Handling Nasty Customers

Nasty customers are a fact of life. Their Prozac supply runs out and they take it out on you. They were unhappy with their last purchase, and the next thing you know, they are beating up on you. It doesn't matter if you are a rookie or a pro. You could be young or old, male or female. Just look at nasty customers the wrong way and they will let you have it with both barrels. Answer their objections and alleviate their dissatisfaction, or they will reload and let you have it again. These are customers who spit, steam, and sometimes use four-letter words. They try to intimidate, love to complain, and may get out of control. They are the ones who say things like:

(1) "You apparently don't know what you're talking about."
(2) "Your competition is much cheaper. I'm surprised anyone buys from you."
(3) "It is a wonder you're still in business."
(4) "I never pay sales tax, and I certainly am not going to pay what you ask."
(5) "Where was your last job? McDonald's?"

Nasty customers are worse than tough customers. Tough customers make you earn their business. Nasty customers make you wish you had never crossed their paths. They can be rude, intimidating, manipulative, mean, vulgar, and as many other less-than-complimentary adjectives as you can fit into a sentence. Nasty customers come in all ages, sizes, and walks of life. If you've never encountered a nasty customer, go on to the next page and just wait until your time comes—because it will. If you do have an occasional run-in with Mr. or Ms. Nasty, here are some common misconceptions you might want to think about.

Misconception No. 1: The Customer Is Always Right

False. Nasty customers may lie. Just because they told you they could get the same thing a lot cheaper from someone else doesn't mean that they can. They just want to see if they can play with your head or bargain with you. If you know what is right, stick to your guns. Nasty customers *can* be wrong.

Misconception No. 2: Never Be Ignorant or Arrogant

False. With nasty, arrogant customers, you can afford to be arrogant as well. You can also be ignorant to their demands. You can be ignorant or you can be arrogant, but you can't be both at the same time. If you are both, you might turn into a "nasty" yourself.

Misconception No. 3: Customer Satisfaction Means Customer Loyalty

Bull. Just because nasty customers are satisfied doesn't mean they are coming back. Only loyal customers come back. The trick is to switch that satisfaction into loyalty. But what if you don't want them to come back? What if they are too much of a hassle to deal with for the few bucks they spend? You decide. You are in control. Effectively handling any customer means being in the driver's seat.

Misconception No. 4: You Get What You Give

Uh-uh. Nasty customers can be opportunists. Gimme, gimme, gimme. They want better terms, lower prices, and anything else they can have. Give them an inch and they take two miles. Don't expect to get back as much as you lay out for nasty customers. They always want to be one up.

Misconception No. 5: Price Shoppers Always Buy on Price

Nope. They like to think that they are the world's best negotiators. They brag about "buying at cost," "spending less than wholesale," "beating salespeople into the ground," or "getting things thrown in for free." The truth is, nasty customers like to give that perception, although it is not at all reality. They will bend when shown that benefits far outweigh the price and that service is a necessity rather than an option. Price shoppers need to hear no, rather than "Okay, I will take your offer." They will pay your price if their need is great enough. It is up to you to develop that need.

Misconception No. 6: Nasty Customers Are Nasty People

Sometimes true. Mostly false. All nasty customers have a soft spot somewhere. You have to find it. Get them to smile. Get them to laugh. Say nice things about their mothers. Find out if they like flowers. Do they have small children or grandchildren? Do they have a favorite charity? Get them to open up. Get some emotion. Be their friend. It is tough to be nasty to someone who wants you to like him or her.

Forget your product and price list for a minute and concentrate on a little customer rapport.

The funny thing about nasty customers is that they usually know they are nasty. It is part of their personalities. Sometimes you have to level out the playing field and not try to beat them at their own game, and have their game end in a draw. You need them to buy from you and feel good about it at the same time. Don't succumb to nasty customers. Don't lie down and play dead. Make it a game. Get their money and get a smile out of them at the same time. Make them glad they had a chance to deal with you. Turn a "whiner" into a "winner" and get a sale.

14

Maintaining Control of Your Customer

When someone brings in an instrument from a mail-order catalog for repair, do you tell him to box it up and send it back to where he bought it? Do you tell him what he can do with his instrument and his catalog? When you find out the person you tried to sell a $2,000 guitar to bought it down the street, do you treat him like dirt when he comes in for strings? When a customer buys a grand piano from your competition and comes to you for lessons, do you spit and tell her to take her lessons there as well? That will show them.

Trouble is, they will tell everyone they know. Maybe they were actually unhappy with the services where they did business and wanted to give you another chance. Maybe they would trade their instruments in with you after a while. Maybe they would turn into regular accessory or print music customers, and refer their friends and relatives. Maybe you could make a few bucks on service, make a friend, and create a great impression, so much so that they would help drive business into your store.

The big discount stores come and go. Same goes for smaller retailers. If you want to compete and survive, attitude and customer service are going to be a major force. Prices alone will not do it. If you can't compete on price all of the time, compete on a level where your competition doesn't stand a chance. What are your strong points? Figure it out. Be nice. Fuming over a lost sale to a bigger competitor is not going to strengthen your business. Complaining about other retailers "giving the stuff away" will only create more traffic for them, not you. Capitalizing on what you do well, things that your competition can't compete with, will increase your margins and build your business. It could be through repairs, lessons, accessories, sheet music, inventory selection, technical expertise, music knowledge—whatever. A "told you so" attitude won't make a friend. Friends make good customers. A "what can I do to help" approach after a customer rebounds from your competition might just put more money in your cash register.

Responsibility. That is what selling takes. It is a necessary element. Have you ever had the experience where you are out shopping for a particular item and the salesperson seems to be almost totally oblivious to what is going on? You ask a question, and the answers could just as well have come out of a computer. The salesperson is disinterested. *You* are in control. You make the decision about whether to buy the product or service without any input from anyone else. In fact, you could be downright rude to some salespeople and they would have stock answers to anything you threw at them. It is not so much that they keep their cool—it is more like their job is a chore. Their attitude is: "Hurry up so I can go home." Or maybe you know more about the product than the salesperson does, and he is just going along for the ride hoping that you will buy it.

Sometimes salespeople don't even ask if you want to buy it or not. Makes you want to go somewhere else, doesn't it?

Have you ever gone into a music store as a customer and felt like you were an intrusion on the salesperson's day? Or have you encountered a salesperson who gave you a great demo, then let you walk out of the store without ever asking you to buy?

Then there are the salespeople who do such a good job of presenting features and benefits that you can't wait to buy whatever they are selling. It is amazing what can happen when a salesperson exercises enough control to make a sale, yet not so much that the customer feels pressured, manipulated, or overwhelmed.

The next time you talk to a customer, think about who is in control. Is it you, or is the customer trying to make you jump through hoops? Are you in charge and trying to make every sale, or are you letting people walk out of the door without your best effort? Could your sales numbers be improved by increasing your control factor?

Responsibility and control go hand in hand. Responsibility is a great quality to have as a salesperson, and it's a great asset to have out of the store as well.

15

Never Embarrass Your Customers

Have you ever had customers come into your store who were so misinformed, it took a great effort to not laugh? It took all of your control for your jaw not to hit the floor at their completely uneducated questions or statements? You might not have said so at the time, but you were thinking it. We all have, on occasion. The problem is that even though it might not come out of your mouth, they can still sense it, and they get embarrassed. It might not happen all the time, but even once is too much. Here are five things *not* to do, so that customers will not feel embarrassed.

Don't Laugh at Them

If they don't know a lot about your instrument and expect it to cost half of what you're selling it for, you're going to have to get them to be your friend before going any further. Be nice. Put yourself in their shoes. How would you feel if you wanted something out of your price range? Explain financing and credit options. Explain features and benefits. Explain *why* it costs what it does. Give them a little education like a good neighbor. Even if they decide not to buy it, they may send other customers to you. You never know.

Don't Make Customers Feel Stupid

Talk in terms they understand. Don't talk over their heads. Stay away from industry jargon they might not be familiar with. Use one- and two-syllable words, but don't go to the other extreme and start talking in a condescending tone. Your customer could be a neurosurgeon for all you know. So just because she gave you a blank stare when you brought up that digital piano's voicing capability, it doesn't mean she's an idiot. Remember: the more comfortable you can make your customers, the more apt they are to do business with you.

Don't Be a Jerk

Don't talk to other salespeople about your customers in front of them, as if they weren't there. Customers who feel they are the salesperson's source of entertainment for the day will seldom buy. And they make sure nobody else will either, guaranteed.

Don't Walk Away from Them Like They Are Not There

Okay. They said they just wanted to look. Maybe the last five customers said the same thing and walked out without buying anything. Whose fault was that? Should you take it out on the ones presently in the store? Be courteous and try to engage them in conversation. You never know what might trigger some positive response.

Never Judge Customers' Stations in Life by Their Looks or Their Clothes

A customer may look like a panhandler but have thousands of dollars in his pocket and 25 years as a classical pianist. Maybe she drives an old jalopy and has threadbare clothes, but also has a PhD in music education and excellent credit. It's easy to think: "They're out of their league." Assume they're not, and make it your business to find out. Look for the silver lining.

One of the problems we have in the music business is that we know a lot. We play. Some of us are even talented. We know the technical side of instruments and love to dazzle customers with our expertise. At least a lot of us do. Nothing can be more fun than talking about customers after they leave our store. "They wanted a Fender Strat for two hundred bucks. They looked like they couldn't afford a set of strings." "This guy was nuts. I showed him. Told him to go down the street."

Maybe sometimes we have to get it out of our systems. It's when we get it out of our systems in front of the customer that's the problem. So hold it in. Smile whether you want to or not. Be polite, be courteous, and don't start with the intimidating, demeaning words and phrases. And don't talk to the customer as if she has an IQ of 36. Don't embarrass the person doing the buying; it can be an easy thing to do. The hardest part is that sometimes you don't know you're doing it. Be careful. A little tact can go a long way.

16

Going Head to Head with Your Online Competitors

This is a common problem today. A customer says, "We're going to think about it," and you know darn well they are going to go home and check the Internet for the lowest price. It's a tough situation. It's hard competing on price or convenience when it comes to your Internet-based competitors. Online retailers are open 24 hours a day, 7 days a week. You can browse the store and purchase an instrument or music accessories from the comfort of your home, office, or anywhere you can get a connection. And with lower overheads, Internet prices are many times lower than in-store prices.

So how can you compete against such a dominant force? The first thing is to make sure you have a competitive website that will get people to come into your store. Then it comes down to simply engaging the customer with human interaction and a great personal experience.

Even though the Internet is high tech and convenient, it can also be a cold, dark place. You can kind of compare it to having a romantic dinner with a robot. The personal, human interaction with sensitivity and feeling is just not there. So when you come up against a customer who is going to go home and buy your instrument cheaper online, there are some things to consider before you just lie down and play dead.

Making the customer feel important and valued is one clear advantage that traditional music instrument retailers have over online stores. You need an informative staff that can help instruct, engage, and create a bond with the customer. This is difficult to do online but easy to do within a bricks-and-mortar store. You need to have your salespeople ramp up their personalities and sales skills. Good marketing strategies and strong promotions will increase the number of customers who come through your door, but if your sales staff do not have the ability to convert prospects into customers, then their efforts are wasted. The ability to connect with the customer is essential when selling a musical instrument, and this comes down to asking the right questions, developing rapport, and providing helpful solutions.

You need to sell the unique experience of being in your store, not just the prices. We have a nation of bargain hunters who are now more price savvy than ever before. However, customers don't just buy on price; otherwise, we'd all be buying everything secondhand on eBay and Craigslist. What do you have that online retailers can't compete with? Lessons? Repairs? Rentals? Hands-on demos?

Also, communication is a key factor. Staying in your customer's face is vital to building a long-term relationship and establishing music-store loyalty. E-newsletters are an easy, low-cost, and instant form of communication, but they are not really the best strategy for a traditional Main Street music retailer who is competing with online competitors. Sending out an e-mail blast or running an ad once in a while rarely generates business. Music stores must maintain regular contact with prospects and customers. *Frequency* is the most effective method of building and engaging relationships with people we want to do more business with.

Direct mail catalogues, informative product guides, and even just a thank-you card in the mail can be far more effective. There is such a thing as "law of reciprocity," where a positive action is responded to with an equally positive reaction. Think about it. If someone buys you a drink at a bar and then has to rush off before you can buy him one back, you feel uncomfortable—the balance is out of kilter. Most people will feel the need to return the favor and remember to buy the first round as soon as they meet up again.

Retail marketing can work the same way. Sending free gifts to customers (even something as small as a couple of guitar picks or a lottery ticket) will more often than not generate the need for them to give you something back in the form of a purchase or at least a visit to your store.

Don't try to fight fire with fire. Avoid discounting. Discounting a price merely reduces its perceived value and makes it difficult to ever sell that item again at its full original price. To compete, try adding value instead by bundling an instrument with another item or accessory. You can also talk up your service, or trade-in policy, after the sale.

It costs up to 20 times as much to get new customers as it does to keep the ones you've got. You need to have a maintenance program in place to keep your customers. This can include thank-you cards, social media, an occasional free gift, e-mails, special offers, and follow-up phone calls. The number of ways to follow up with your customers is endless. If your music store does not have a maintenance-marketing plan in place, then it is at risk of losing current customers.

17

Qualifying Means Developing Listening Skills

It is important that we find out as much about our customers' needs as possible. We also want to answer any objections that they might have. When assessing needs and answering objections, remember: you have two ears and one mouth. Use them in that proportion. The person who does the most of the talking ends up with the instrument. If you do most of the talking, you end up with what you were trying to sell.

The key to creative qualifying is asking the right questions and then listening to the answers so you can figure out which way to go about selling to your customers. Here are a few things you might want to find out:

(1) What brings them into your store today?
(2) Have they been here before?
(3) If so, whom have they spoken with?
(4) Are they looking for products for themselves or to give as gifts?
(5) What instrument(s) do they play?
(6) Are they beginners, hobbyists, serious students, or seasoned professionals?
(7) If they are professionals, do they play locally?

(8) Have they taken lessons?

(9) Are they local, or did they come from a distance?

(10) Have they shopped somewhere already?

(11) What have they seen that they really like?

(12) Why didn't they purchase it?

(13) Would financing help in their decision to buy an instrument(s)?

(14) Do they have a trade?

(15) What instrument(s) have they owned in the past?

The higher priced the instrument, the more things you might want to find out about your customers. Get them to be your friends. Get into a conversation about their likes and dislikes. You will be amazed by how much you can find out and how this information can help you make a sale.

Here is something else to think about. Do you ever ask what type of music your customers like to play or listen to? Do you demo with your own Top-10 repertoire of hits, thinking that since you like it, your customers better like it too? Find out if they are into golden oldies, classic rock, Christian rock, country, jazz, and so forth. Then demo according to their tastes, not yours.

The more you know about your customers, the easier it will be to get them to spend money in your store. Establish some rapport. Get them to like you. Remember: If they like you, they are more apt to trust you. If they trust you, it is definitely much easier to get them to buy. It starts with qualifying, and qualifying means listening to what they have to say.

18

Product Knowledge Versus Sales Knowledge

Far too many retail music employees (owners and sales staff alike) believe product-knowledge training is sales training. Product knowledge definitely has its place. You need to know all about the instruments you're selling. When retail music salespeople know their products inside and out, and can demonstrate the features and benefits to the customer, it goes a long way toward leading that customer to buy. However, it's going to take more than product knowledge to sell to many customers. You need to know more than the basics of selling. You need to combine product knowledge with sales strengths, creativity, ambition, common sense, decent persistence, personality, conversational skills, and a positive attitude. Whew! That's a lot, isn't it?

If you're in the retail music business, chances are you like music. You might be a musician. You might play out. You might have given lessons. You probably already have a lot of instrument product knowledge inside your head. Maybe you don't like the thought of "selling." You'd much rather have the customer "buy."

Okay, but if you don't use some sales smarts, you're simply a clerk rather than a salesperson. If you're a commissioned salesperson, sales knowledge is not just an option, it is a necessity. There are a lot of points in this book dedicated to sales ideas and increasing your sales strengths. The most important thing, however, is to believe that it is necessary, and combine those sales ideas you like the best with your musical instrument expertise.

If you don't like selling, you're in the wrong business. You need to determine that now. Some of the best salespeople in the music industry can't play a note and are still tremendously successful. If you can play, already have a broad knowledge of instruments and product knowledge, and can couple those skills with sales techniques, you are way ahead of the pack.

Never stop learning. That goes for both product knowledge and sales knowledge. When you're green, you're growing; when you're ripe, you rot. Always look for the next idea you can put to use to accelerate your career. The music business is a fun business. Selling more makes it more fun!

19

Closing 101: Asking for the Sale

Uh-oh, closing. If you can't close, nothing else you do right matters. You don't need to be slick. You just need to be yourself, know what you are talking about, create some positive acceptance, and just simply ask: "Would you like to get it?" It's not that hard. If you don't ask, you don't get. Let your salespeople know that. They need to ask the customers to buy.

A lot of the time, the real key to selling is: you ask, you get. Sometimes the more you ask, the more you get. Some people are terrible at presentations, horrible at qualifying, and the worst at customer rapport—but they're great askers. Obviously, presenting, qualifying, and rapport are important, but if you could take advantage of being competent in all of these areas and learn to ask, too, you'd be invincible.

One reason many salespeople don't ask for the order is that they don't know *when* to ask. J. Douglas Edwards, sales guru from years gone by, used to say, "The only way you'll ever learn to close is to close early, close often, and close hard." Baloney. Salespeople who hammer the customer continually learn sooner or later that closing hurts. Rejection is hard to take. Hearing no is not fun. Mark Twain once said, "If a cat sits on a hot stove and gets burned, it'll never sit on another hot stove again. In fact, it will never sit on a cold stove either. It's out of the business of sitting on stoves, period."

If we are rejected every time we close, sooner or later we're not going to want to close anymore. If we get burned enough times, we start to get burned out. In every successful sale, there's a right time and a wrong time to close. You have to learn to watch for that right time. Close too early, and you'll get an objection or a stall. Close too late, and you could talk your way out of a sale.

Selling musical instruments can be a matter of asking a customer to buy at the right time. Establishing customer confidence and customer trust makes it easier for you when you ask a customer to buy. In fact, it kind of extends the closing time. It gives you a wider window. Once that window is shut, you hear things like: "I'll think it over, give me your card," "Let me talk it over with my banker," "I don't think I can afford it," "Let me talk to my wife about it," ad nauseam. We've all been there.

So the key to this whole closing thing is:

(1) Knowing when to ask.
(2) Actually asking.
(3) Keeping in synch with your customers all the while.

The last one is more like being in stride with them, pacing them, and occasionally matching their mannerisms. Think about it like trying to jump aboard a slow-moving freight train. You run alongside of it for a bit until you get in stride with the train. Then you reach up with one hand and grab a rung on the ladder while you are still running. Then you reach up with the other hand while you run along with it some more and finally jump up and on . . . gently. If you don't have the guts to jump up, you get left behind. If you don't match the speed of the train while you are running, you get left behind. If you run too fast and the train is barely moving, you lose your opportunity as well. Selling is exactly the same.

If you've been in the music business for any period of time, you've probably been to a sales training seminar or two, maybe watched a couple of videos on selling, and read several books on closing sales. Many of these programs immediately take for granted the fact that the customer doesn't really *want* to buy what you're selling, yet they still offer idea after idea on how to get the person to buy. They even name the closes. There's the "Ben Franklin Close," the "Right-Angle Close," the "Sharp-Angle Close," and the "Crash-and-Burn Close." That's not to be confused with the "I'll-Think-It-Over Close" and the "If-I-Can-Would-You Close." And that's only the beginning. They go on forever.

I'll bet any salesperson could double his or her sales starting tomorrow morning by just asking everyone he or she gave a demo to to buy the instrument. "Call me when you're ready" doesn't count. "Here's my card" doesn't make it. "Whatcha' think?" doesn't quite do it either. It's really easy. You don't need 50 different closes. You just need to be yourself and simply ask, "Can I write it up?" Even a simple "Okay with you?" might work.

To be a supersalesperson, a real star, you just have to find a need and fill it, and then have the guts to ask for the sale (along with the decent persistence to ask several times, maybe several different ways). Don't justify not asking because you assume that the customer won't buy. Don't make the decision for the customer unless it's a positive decision. Many customers need a little push. The best analogy is *a cow doesn't give milk; you have to take it from her.* Customers come into your store with your money in their pockets. The idea is to get the money from their pockets to your pocket. It's kind of like a game. If they buy, you win. If they walk, you lose. You can't win every time. Nobody can. Don't take losing a sale as a personal rejection. Losing a sale is not the end of the world. Not asking for the sale and having a customer walk is.

Forget the volumes of books on closing. They won't help if you don't know your products inside and out, if you don't ask customers to buy, and if you don't use a little decent persistence in case they waiver. Also, you have to treat them with respect and as friends. Remember, people are more apt to buy from someone they like. It's that easy.

(8) "They said up front they weren't really in the market, but
    just wanted to get some information in case they ever were
    interested in buying."
(9) "I was really busy and had other customers at the same time."
(10) "I knew they could buy it down the street for less."

The list could go on. But let's take a look at the 38 percent who ask
every customer to buy. There's probably an equally long list of why
they ask for a sale, but I bet the No. 1 reason is this: they aren't afraid
to hear no. They can handle rejection. They're used to it. They can
deal with it. But a lot of salespeople can't. Hearing "No, I don't want
it" is hard, and sometimes salespeople look at it as embarrassing and
demeaning. But let's face it, not everyone is going to buy from you all
of the time. You are going to be rejected every once in a while.

The rule of thumb is this: *don't ever want a sale so badly that you
are afraid to ask the customer to buy.* If you start hoping customers will
say "I'll take it" before you have to ask, they may walk out of the door
first. If you want to have your sales increase dramatically, stop thinking about *whether* you are going to ask and start thinking about *when.*
Think about how you ask. Are you still using the closing techniques
of 30 years ago? Maybe it's time to throw away the sales manuals
and cassette tapes that tell you to "think positive, put your best foot
forward, and know at least 75 closes."

Start asking your customers to buy at the first sign of positive acceptance. When they say, "I love that sound," just say, "Great, would
you like to get it?" Keep asking the customer to buy all the way through
your demo and the customer might just say, "I want it." If you ask
things during your demo like "Isn't this what you want?" "Do you
like the color?" "Could you use this right away?" or "Would it work
for you?" you will never have to fear rejection, because you will know
where you stand all the way along. If you start to get a lot of negative
feedback, you'll know that you have to shift gears before you ask the
customer to buy. If you get a lot of positive responses, you'll know

that can you ask the customer to buy quickly. Not knowing where you stand can make it hard to ask for a sale, because "rejection" might rear its ugly head. Keep this in mind: Customers probably won't say no and berate you. They probably won't say no and run out the door.

The other secret to handling rejection is this: *don't ever take losing a sale personally.*

You can't sell to everybody, and prospects will come and go all day long. It's a numbers game. It's like going bear hunting. Sometimes you get the bear, and sometimes the bear gets you. But the nice part about selling is that you get to do it again and again. Sure, rejection is hard to take, but if you make asking for a sale a simple, easy process (instead of a challenge), you'll find the response "I'll take it" will far surpass "Give me your card; I want to think about it." Eventually, the occasional rejection will go right over your head. It's good to get your fanny kicked once in a while. It makes you humble. Two no's in a row might mean you'll get eight yesses right after that. And if you don't ask, you'll never know. Don't worry about rejection. You'll get the sale the next time around.

21

The Little-Harder Sell

No one likes to get his or her arm twisted into buying something. Forget about using "pressure" to sell. No one likes pressure. Wait a minute; let's think about it. What is "high pressure" anyway? Here is the answer: If customers thinks that it's pressure, then it is pressure. If they don't think it's pressure, then it's not. It's all in the mind of the beholder.

After you've qualified, listened, demonstrated, and tried the simple closes mentioned in the previous section, such as:

(1) "Would you like to get it?"
(2) "Okay with you?"
(3) "Want to take it with you?"

... and you still can't crack the sale, you might want to sit customers down if it is a high-priced instrument, since nobody buys anything big standing up (you didn't buy your car or house standing up, did you?) Reason with customers. Maybe you can ask directly, "Is there any reason you're not getting this right now?" See what they say. Remember, you have to shut up and listen. It is very easy to just jump in without hearing the full objection and try to answer it before all the words come out of their mouths.

Get your customers to talk. Listen with both ears. Make sure they like you and trust you. Then you can get specific. Ask if they are going to check the Internet, look around, or maybe they just don't like the instrument, period. Find out the real reasons they aren't buying, try to overcome whatever objections they come back with, and then *ask*. If that doesn't work, get them to talk some more, and *ask again*.

Don't give up. Get them to laugh with you. Find some common denominator where you can share similar experiences. Maybe you play the same instrument, are from the same town, drive the same car, have seen the same movies or read the same books. The idea here is to just get them to talk. Get them to open up. Let them know this is how you make your living and they are important to you. Get them to talk freely.

You never know if they will just talk themselves into the sale. You never know unless you try.

Here's another thing to think about: Maybe they won't buy the first time around. Maybe you can get them back in again. Maybe they will think of something else they need and think of you and your store.

Don't give up. If they don't buy right then, maybe they will buy later. That's why you need to be their friend and instill their confidence in you and your store.

22

What to Do If Your Customer Walks

You're not going to sell to everybody and not everybody is going to like you. Not every customer will buy the first time around. Usually the main reasons customers leave without buying are:

(1) No need.
(2) No trust.
(3) No money.

If they don't need it, there's no way around it. But maybe they will need it later or maybe they will have a friend who needs it. The key here is to keep them on your list of people whom you might want to stay in touch with. They could refer their friends. You never know.

If they don't trust you, they probably won't buy from you unless your price is ridiculously low, and even then they might be suspect. If they like you, they will trust you and have confidence in you. If they trust you, there's a good chance they will buy from you. Think about how you could get them back and instill that trust. Maybe you could bring them back by asking for their opinion on something new that just came on the market. People love to give opinions. Showing you have confidence in them might build their trust in you.

If they have no credit or no money, the point is moot. Maybe they will have credit or money later, but the idea here is to not belabor the situation, and simply concentrate on the next customer who walks through the door. We can't sell to everybody, but we can sell to a lot of customers if we just think clearly and try to analyze each situation individually.

Don't think of those customers who get away without buying as a lost cause. Look at it more in a positive light. Think of what you may have learned from the experience, if you made any mistakes during the sale, and how you can avoid those missteps the next time. Then think of what you can do to get them back in one more time. Maybe you could send them an e-mail or text. That's why it is important to get information such as cell phone numbers and e-mail addresses. Maybe you could have your customers fill out "valued customer cards" with some contact information. Then put those people on your own e-mail list.

Everyone who walks should be on your list. Send out a blast every once in a while. Maybe a text like: "got good news for u. give me a call." Then try to get them back in. You never know who might come back through your door. Call them on the phone if you have their numbers. Stay in touch. Make the most out of all customers, whether they buy or not. Customers who don't buy today might come back to buy tomorrow, next week, next month, or next year.

They also might refer their friends.

23

Selling for Margin

You're in business to make a profit. You are not a providing a public service to your community by giving instruments away. Sometimes customers want to try to negotiate by offering us ridiculous prices for what we are selling. Explain that this is how you stay in business, and you want to *earn* their business. Again, get them to be your friends. Let them know you want them to come back time and time again.

You might want to bundle certain instruments so they look different to compare and so that there is perceived value. Maybe include music and lessons when talking with a customer, depending on the instrument and his or her reasons for buying.

One easy way to create more margin is by being careful when customers ask, "Is that the best you can do?"

When this happens, what do you say? Think about it. Do you say, "Let me check with my manager?" Do you offer to include the sales tax, or do you drop it a few bucks, hoping they will buy it right then?

When customers ask, "Is that the best you can do?" there is only one answer:

Yes.

Who knows, the customer might just say, "Okay, I'll take it." If you drop the price right away just to get the sale quicker, you might be losing a lot of margin.

Here's something else to consider: What do you do with the customer who likes the instrument and seems to be on your side, then says, "I can buy it cheaper down the street [or online]"? How do you know that for a fact? Is he just making it up? Can we check online and show him that what he sees may not be what he gets? Does that instrument include lessons, accessories, trade-in guarantee, music, or whatever else your store might be famous for? Is that competitive price from across town really just in your customer's head?

Again, analyze each situation as it comes up. Think about what you are doing and how much margin can be obtained with every sale.

Selling can be a bit like a game. The customer has your money in her pocket. The trick is to get it from her pocket to your register. Don't be too anxious to start cutting price. Before long you will be below cost if the customer knows she has the advantage by beating you up over price.

So when a customer asks if that is the best you can do, simply say yes and see what the customer says. He or she might just go out the door with the instrument at the price you were looking for.

24

Finding Your Own Customers

If you've been in the music business for any length of time, you've probably noticed that every once in a while, things start to get a little slow. It's not gangbusters every day of the week, every week of the year. Maybe it's the weather, the economy, vacations, the season, or any number of variables that can affect sales revenue. So, what do you do when business starts to soften? Come up with a new promotion? Run some advertising? Do a mailing campaign?

Great, but these ideas are only good if they actually catch interest and don't cost more than you bring in. If your sales start to go into tilt and you don't have a hefty advertising budget, times could get a little tough. There is some marketing you can do, however, without spending serious cash. How about looking to your staff for some ideas or talking to your salespeople, or even your administrative personnel, about their thoughts for finding more customers? Could they be of any help? It might not be a bad idea to have a meeting with everyone in your store to ask for their input. See if they have any ideas on how you can get more people to walk through your door. You might be amazed when the lowest paid person on your payroll comes up with an idea or two.

Of course, a lot depends on what type of music store you have (full line, band instruments, combo, pianos, etc.) and whether you have commissioned salespeople. Seven-dollar-an-hour clerks might come up with a few ideas, but after that, they probably will leave it up to you to get more floor traffic. On the other hand, if you have salespeople who work on any type of commission, it definitely will be in their best interest to get everyone involved in creating more customers.

A music store with proactive salespeople, who can help bring customers through the door without relying on media advertising or store promotion, can run rings around competition that is slashing prices and running its third annual "Going Out of Business Sale." It's *okay* to be reactive and wait for the next customer to come through the door, but how many more gross sales could you be generating if your salespeople could bring in their own people?

Generating traffic without a huge ad budget is possible. Car dealers and insurance agencies do it all the time. Real estate people do it too. Here are some suggestions that you and your salespeople can utilize to generate more business.

The basics:

Make Every Incoming Phone Call Count

When people call looking for information about a musical instrument, get their names before giving a price. Use their names during the conversation. It's easy. Just say, "This is [your name]; with whom am I speaking?" Then try to get them into the store. Put them on your mailing list. Stay in touch with them.

Business Cards (When Put to Use) Can Bring In More Business

Everyone in your store should have his or her own card. Invent titles for your employees if you have to. Make sure they have cards with them at all times to give out to their circle of influence—anywhere, anytime. Tell your employees to use them at parties, standing in line at the grocery store, at public events—anywhere they might talk with others. Besides, business cards help give your employees pride in where they work.

Personal Promotion Is Important

Commissioned salespeople should send out a few notes or postcards each day to past customers urging them to stop by and see them personally about new items. The cards could say something as simple as, "Trying to reach you, give me a call." Ten cards a day is a good target, and the process will only take a few minutes.

Make Cold Calls

If sending out cards is too much, salespeople should call some of their friends, relatives, acquaintances, past customers, new customers, or prospective customers each day. A half a dozen calls a day ought to do it. Tell them about a new instrument that just came in that you'd like to get their opinions on. You will be amazed how many people like to give their opinions, and how many will come into the store to do it. These calls could be made first thing in the morning. If the caller gets voice mail, he or she might leave a message saying, "This is [salesperson's name] at [your music store]. I've got good news for you. Please give me a call." Everyone likes good news, and your news could be a special price on a new instrument, or anything that might trigger response.

Use Your E-Mail List

All salespeople should have their own e-mail address list of personal contacts who are interested in music. If you are not sure what to put in your e-mail, come up with some data about the instruments you carry and send out an interesting fact or two each week to your list. Urgency at the end about why the prospect should come to the store ("Limited Time Offer," "Only One Remaining," etc.) is a good idea.

The "Who Do You Know" List

Where do you look for more prospects and customers when there's no one left to talk to? Everyone has his or her own circle of influence. These are the people you go to, not just for business, but for referrals as well. Keep in touch with these people on a regular basis to increase your day-to-day traffic.

Who do you know . . .

(1) From your old job?
(2) From school?
(3) Through your kids?
(4) Whom you play golf with?
(5) Whom you hunt or fish with?
(6) Who has sold you something (suits, cars, glasses, etc.)?
(7) Who has sent you a letter recently?
(8) Whom you have written a check to this year?
(9) Who owns your local hardware, grocery, shoe, or furniture store?
(10) Who is your lawyer, hairdresser, florist, dentist, doctor, jeweler, or realtor?
(11) Who is on your Christmas list?
(12) Who manages your local movie theater, bank, or fitness club?
(13) Who was at your wedding?
(14) Who took your family photos?
(15) Who is a new neighbor?

There is no limit to the people in your center of influence, in your circle of influence, and who just pass through your life. These are your contacts. These are the people you want to stay in touch with. You never know when they might need a new musical instrument, accessories, or simply advice. You want to keep customers coming through your door all day long. It starts with keeping in touch.

25

Thank-You Notes

Have you ever said to one of your customers, "I know you come in here a lot, and I just wanted to tell you that I really appreciate your business"? Or do you sort of take your customers for granted, figuring that they won't go anyplace else—and since "thank you" is printed on every receipt, that's enough of a show of appreciation for the moment?

Try reversing the situation. Do you ever do business with someone who doesn't care one way or another if you do business with him or not? How do you feel? I'll bet you probably don't care that much about doing business with him on a regular basis either, if at all.

Customers do repeat business with stores or dealerships where they are satisfied each time they visit. But sometimes even satisfied customers will slip away. If someone else can satisfy them more, they might start doing business down the street.

That's where the thank-you notes, the personal attention, the genuine appreciation for their business comes in. Do you let your customers know that you really appreciate them, or are you just taking it for granted that since you're a great music store, they're always going to be there? If you don't make an effort to express your appreciation, one of these days they just might stop coming in.

So, do you send thank-you notes to your customers? Do you write "Thank You!" on the invoices and sign your name? Do you even have the time? Probably not. You have more to do than writing thank-you notes to people you've already sold to. They're already customers. You said thank you when you rang up or wrote up their sales. If we're going to write to people, we usually only think to contact our current customers with sale flyers, bills, new product information, and regular customer mailings. But notes just to say thank you? C'mon. Wal-Mart doesn't. Price Club doesn't. And there is the point.

You want to be different from your competitors. You want to develop the fine art of "faceting." It's the facets that give a diamond its sparkle and appeal. It's the same with your business. Find different ways to appeal to your customers, to present your instruments, and to develop and sustain customer interest. You want to be different from all the other retailers, with your own personal look and image. You want to be unique and interesting. Nothing is easier to ignore than a boring business.

People like to feel appreciated. With so many businesses today seemingly more concerned with bringing in new customers and making a quick sale than following up and keeping their current customers happy, a quick thank-you note may be just the thing to make your customers feel valued.

The music business is different from some other retailers in the sense that you sell fun, enjoyment, entertainment, and a sense of accomplishment on a day-to-day basis. Maybe you did say thank you when you sold your last guitar, set of drums, or keyboard. But what if you sent your customers a handwritten note saying that you appreciated their business? And since this is how you make your living, you'd also appreciate it if they mentioned your name and the name of your store to their friends?

If you really want to create more business for your store without spending huge amounts on additional advertising, maybe you could start with your current customer base. Think about what the function of your business is. The function of your business is not to make a profit. The *goal* of your business is to make a profit. When we start to confuse the function with the goal is when we start to have a bit of a problem. The function of your music business is to create and maintain customers. *Maintain* is the key word. Keep them coming back. Friends like to buy from friends. They buy from people they trust. If people like and trust you and your staff, sometimes price and product knowledge are secondary. That human element of sincerity and appreciation is tough to compete with. It's a great way not only to increase your business but to increase your profit margins as well.

So think about it. Maybe you can't send a thank you note to everyone who buys a couple of guitar picks, a set of strings, or some sheet music. But if you spend some serious time with a customer who ends up spending a lot of money (and you get to know him by name), and you find out about his musical expertise and his likes and dislikes (and he knows you as more than a faceless clerk), maybe it would be a good time to extend a second thank-you. A note to his home. A note that asks him to come back again to see you personally. What if 40 percent of those customers came back to buy something else from you within 30 days and referred you to their friends as well? Maybe you'd have to build a bigger store. You never know.

26

A Personal Approach to Direct Mail

E-Mail Versus Direct Mail: Which Reaches Your Customers Better?

Not so long ago, only a few people had e-mail addresses. Now, no self-respecting computer owner (and that's just about everybody) would be without one. Sure, a small number of people still have rotary phones, but even these folks can have an e-mail account. In fact, just about every age group has e-mail. Five-year-olds have it, as well as 95-year-olds. E-mail is cheap. You can send out letters to your e-mail list as many times as you want without huge postage costs.

Just a few years ago, many music retailers abandoned direct mail almost overnight in favor of e-mail and websites. There seemed to be a massive migration toward electronic marketing. E-mail "blasting" could reach tens of thousands of buyers at a fraction of the cost of direct mail. And it was quick and easy to implement. However, since every single company seemed to be doing it, consumers haven't taken e-mail as seriously as direct mail. Constant bombardment from tens (if not hundreds) of thousands of spam operations has been too much for many customers to bear. E-mail started to be intrusive. Today you have to compete with Nigerian money scams, Viagra at giveaway prices, stock hypes, porn sites, and prescription-drug mail-order firms. You also have to compete with e-mail solicitations from big companies such as Pier 1, Best Buy, Circuit City, Amazon, and so on down the list.

Just about everyone takes direct mail seriously. First of all, when the mail arrives, it's one of the most important moments of the day, both at the office and at home. We complain if it's late and feel deprived if there is nothing of any importance. Usually we stop whatever we're doing when the "snail mail" arrives to go through it. In other words, we still view postal mail as a priority. Many people feel slighted when they find out there's nothing in their morning mail at home. It's not exactly the same for e-mail.

Second, postal mail has a more personal feel to it. Most people would much rather receive a Hallmark card in the mail than an electronic greeting card. They're just not the same. More thought and effort goes into sending a card in the mail. We give the most attention to the mail that seems the most personal. We reject the mail that looks like nothing more than an ad. With direct mail, you can easily personalize the envelope, letter, or marketing copy.

Third, regular mail is tangible. You can hold it in your hand. You can feel it. You can toss it in the trash if it's something you don't want, but it takes more than a click to get rid of it. I know people who hang onto direct-mail response cards for months before they send them in. E-mail is designed for instant action, and most of the time it's instant deletion. That's not to say that an e-mail list and e-mail letters don't work. It's just that direct mail seems to work better, in spite of the cost. Sure, you can do both, but an aggressive, well-thought-out direct-mail campaign still seems to bring in more immediate bucks.

Think about this: If you send out an envelope (that has nothing in it) with your return address on the outside and a phone number underneath, stick a stamp on it (rather than running it through the postage meter), and write the word *important* in the bottom left-hand corner, there's a very good chance the person receiving the envelope with nothing inside will call you to see what was in the envelope. (You made it easy with your phone number below the return address.) That's how easy and effective direct mail can be. (Of course when recipients call to ask what was in the envelope, you can tell them about an upcoming sale, concert, or clinic and simply try to get them in the store.) Compare that to e-mail. Send e-mail to someone with no subject line or no message, and it gets deleted in a flash. It becomes one less thing to deal with. Besides, spam filters are grabbing a lot of the messages, even the ones sent to your opt-in list.

Here are a dozen great ideas for direct mail:

(1) A new-product introduction.
(2) The introduction of a new staff member.
(3) Answers to frequently asked questions.
(4) The promotion of a concert or clinic.
(5) A schedule of store events (to hang on the refrigerator).
(6) A last-minute sale or promotion.
(7) Hot products from NAMM (National Association of Music Merchant) shows.
(8) Reminders.
(9) Seasonal specials.
(10) Tips, hints, or helpful information
(11) Thank-yous.
(12) Invitations to any kind of special event.

So don't throw away your customer mailing list in favor of an e-mail list. Continue to update it. Buy a good mailing list once in a while to attract new business. You should continue to use your e-mail list, but don't forget about direct mail. It still has tremendous benefits.

27

Incoming Calls: Your Greatest Source of New Business

As far as incoming calls go, handling those calls correctly could really have a positive impact on your sales. I have addressed this in a number of NAMM university sessions, along with several columns in *The Music Trades* magazine. When I bring it up to some music retailers, I can sense immediately a little distain in their voice. Basically their attitude is, "Don't tell me how to talk on the phone, I've been doing it for years." Well maybe there are a few things you could do differently. For example (as I wrote in *Music Trades*), it's amazing how few music stores ever ask who's calling. As a test, I called 10 music stores last week looking for a specific instrument. I blocked caller ID on my cell phone so my name and number wouldn't come up. All I asked was if they had the instrument in stock and what the price was. Out of 10 calls, seven had the instrument in stock and immediately told me the price when asked. Three didn't have the instrument, but they also didn't try to get me in to see something similar. *No one* asked for my name. No one tried to get me in. One told me he was not the person who handled that department and to call back when she was there. Two stores made me feel like I was an intrusion on their day. They were busy, gave me a price, and that was the end of the conversation. I feel you should have two goals when talking to a caller on the phone:

(1) Get a name, and use that name during the conversation.
(2) Try to get the person into the store.

It's very tough to sell an instrument over the phone. The best you can usually do is try to get customers in to see you personally—face to face. Don't give a price and hang up. Be their friend. Find out a little bit about them and what they are looking for. You're probably not going to sell an expensive guitar, keyboard, or drum set over the phone. Just find out who you're talking to and give them a reason to come in. It's basic, it's simple, and it works.

Do you always ask, "Who am I speaking to?" when handling incoming calls? Do your salespeople? Keep a log next to your phone on every incoming call. Get a name, check caller ID to get a callback number, and see if you can get an e-mail address before you're done. Above all, try to get the customers in your store. Get them to come in, and it will be easy after that.

28

10 Telephone Tips

(1) Focus on the phone call you are about to take. Make a conscious mental shift from your last customer, task, or conversation. Don't answer the phone while you are still talking to someone else.

(2) Take a deep inhale, exhale, and *smile* before you answer the phone. Your smile will come through in your voice even though your caller can't see you.

(3) Put a mirror by the phone if possible to remind yourself to smile and sit or stand straight.

(4) Always give your business name and your name when you answer. Callers want to know they have reached the right place and whom they are talking to.

(5) Speak slowly and articulate your words—especially your greeting. Make sure it doesn't sound like "thisismjrblgky."

(6) Use proper English and avoid slang. You're not chatting with your buddies; you are addressing your business contacts.

(7) Be sure to say thank you at the end of every call. There's always a reason to thank a customer for making the effort to contact your company.

(8) The goodbye is as important as the hello. Make sure callers have finished with everything they want to say before you hang up. Wait for them to say goodbye, and hang up before you replace the receiver.

(9) If you are leaving a message on a customer's voice mail (or anyone's voice mail for that matter), it's especially important that you say your name and the company name clearly. You may even want to spell it if there is any question.

(10) When leaving voice mail messages, leave your return phone number even if you think customers already have it. Make sure you say the number distinctly and *slowly*. Remember they are writing this number down, and it is annoying to have to replay the message several times to get it. Another good trick is to say your name, company name, and telephone number at *both* the beginning and the very end of your message.

29

Getting the Word Out

Using Message Boards, Pennysavers, Neighborhood Newspapers, and Door-Hangers

A pennysaver (or free ads paper, Friday ad, or shopper magazine) is a kind of free community periodical available across the country. Typically published weekly or monthly, they are useful for businesses and private merchants looking to advertise. Frequently, pennysavers are actually called *The Pennysaver* (or *Penny Saver*, *Penny-saver*, or *PennySaver*). They usually contain classified ads, often grouped into an extensive set of categories. Many pennysavers also offer local news and entertainment, as well as generic advice information, various syndicated or locally written columns on various topics of interest, limited comics, and primetime TV listings grids in some papers. The term is widely used in the Northeast, though there are pennysavers elsewhere. Pennysavers are sometimes published by a locally dominant daily newspaper as a brand extension of their publication and feature advertisements published in the same style as the parent newspaper. The best part of pennysavers is that their classifieds are usually free.

Here is some information that retail music salespeople may wish to utilize.

Each week have your employees place their own classified ads under musical instruments with their cell phone numbers listed. Change the instruments weekly with clever headings that attract attention. The idea is to get people to call regarding the specific guitar, amp, keyboard, drum set, and so forth, and get them in the store. This is a great way to move used inventory.

Something else: you can write an article that demonstrates your expertise in your music business, and these pennysavers may run the article as a local news feature. Unique adult lesson programs? New concept in learning to play for kids? Send it to noncompeting newspapers that accept submissions from local experts. Be sure your name, store name, phone number, and a reference to your product or service is included at the end of the article.

You can also use those community message boards in supermarkets, car washes, restaurants, and everywhere people tack their business cards or for-sale ads. You see them in libraries, print shops, hair salons, meeting rooms, and anywhere people gather. Don't just post your business card; make up a four-by-six card with pull-off tabs with your store phone number. Then come up with a funny headline. For example: "Illness Forces Sale. We're sick of looking at this guitar that needs a home. Call now. You won't believe the price." Use some creativity.

Then there are door-hangers for doorknobs. For a weekend event, print a specific offer on door-hangers and place them on doorknobs in your area. This method will produce results in direct proportion to the strength of your offer. You don't have to do this yourself. You can hire the Boy Scouts or a local Little League team to do this as a fundraiser for you. Sit down with your staff and think of all the ways you can use these ideas for getting the word out there.

30

Let's Keep the Pros on Our Side

You know who they are. They come in day after day, week after week. They're the local "pros" who play in the area clubs, local symphonic groups, churches, theaters, and anywhere musicians are paid to play. They buy their gear somewhere. It might as well be from you. Some have attitude, some are nice people, some have chips on their shoulders, and some feel they are the greatest thing since Keith Richards. Doesn't matter.

The key is to make them friends of you and your store. Most of them want (or expect) discounts because they often simply search out the lowest price thinking they can figure out any new instrument or accessory for themselves. They expect some consideration, whether it is price, acknowledgement, or referrals. We need these people. And we need them to buy from us.

How about having them do a clinic or concert in your store? How about asking their advice on a new instrument? How about giving them first chance to try out the latest gear as soon as it comes in the store? How about putting together an "advisory committee" of local pros so they feel special and refer their friends?

How about putting up pictures on your walls of them and their bands with instruments they purchased from you? How about putting up any press material on a bulletin board for "pros" in your store? How about referring them for a gig once in a while? How about having a blank white wall where every local "pro" can sign his or her name and say something nice about your store?

How about partnering with your local AFM—the American Federation of Musicians? Could you offer union musicians a small discount for showing their union cards? Could you use them for clinics or concerts by paying the local scale and having all their union and nonunion buddies come, as well as the general public? (Union musicians are a great source of leads and referrals.)

The ideas here are endless. What you don't want to do is alienate them because they may have bought their last instrument somewhere else, either from another music dealer or online. You don't want these folks bad-mouthing you for any reason, because they also have friends who play and need gear. Of course they go other places. For most of them, music is their life. They like to talk about it with anyone who will listen. If you can find any way to help them in their careers, you will find they will help you promote your music store.

So, let's recap.

(1) Ask their advice.
(2) Get their opinions.
(3) Help them with their careers.
(4) Use them for concerts or clinics if you can.
(5) Try not to tick them off.
(6) Get them to be your friends, and friends of the store.

Above all you want to make your store a destination spot for your local "pros."

31

Selling Up, Selling Down, and Add-Ons

Selling Up

Here's where you could significantly increase sales revenue when talking to customers who are looking for specific instruments. Maybe they have already determined the model and price range, but they don't know what else is available for a little more money. Don't be afraid to show your customers the next model or two higher, regardless of the price. Let them know you are there to offer guidance and assistance. You can always go back to the original instrument, but you never know if they'd like something better.

Selling Down

Maybe a certain instrument is out of a customer's price range. Showing a couple of steps below could show her that her dream instrument is a bargain in the long run. The whole thing here is to establish a little trust with your customers. Help them decide. Selling down often results in selling up, or at least selling the instrument the customer was looking for when he or she came in your store.

Selling Add-Ons

Do you have a "just one more thing" phrase in your sales arsenal when you are writing up a sale? Do you automatically ask about strings, picks, stands, and music when cashing out a guitar? Do you bring up CD/DVD instruction courses, logo-wear, sticks, extra cymbals, or drummers' thrones when selling a set of drums? How about a lamp, a better bench, extra tunings, or music when selling a piano?

There are a ton of add-ons you can suggest if you put your mind to it. If a customer says no right away, you can mention that you're just doing your job. Everyone respects someone who just tries to do his or her job. Maybe you have a lot of business right now, with customers who have to take a number to get waited on when they come in the store, *but* if you need some extra revenue because business is not quite as good as you'd like it to be, simply try to get more dollars out of the customers you already have. Train your employees to try to get "one more thing" sold with every customer. It's not that hard. Customers will generally not buy something else on their own; salespeople have to suggest it. Start being a little creative. Put yourself in your customers' shoes. What would be a neat special add-on, a great little extra that could almost be a necessity, or just something that would be nice to have, that every musician could use? The time to suggest it is when you are writing up or cashing out the sale. That's when customers are most excited about what they are buying. They are in a "spending money" frame of mind, and usually their reluctance level and defenses are not as high as once they get home. Come up with some ideas for your salespeople for mentioning add-on items. All stores are different. Try to be unique. If every customer bought one extra item, no matter how small, you could see a serious increase in revenue by the end of the month. Don't say it's impossible until you give it a try.

Don't take for granted that the customer who comes in for a specific instrument wouldn't like something better. Suggest the next model up or two, and then try for add-ons after the sale is made. McDonald's does it ("You want fries with that?"). The post office does it ("Are you all set for stamps?"). You should do a little suggestive selling too.

32

Following Up After the Sale

This is basic. This is Basic Selling 101, if you will. Once your customers leave your store, you want to make sure they come back again. It's like an airplane engine that is starting up. It's tough to get it to turn over a couple of times, but once it cranks, it keeps going and going and going. You want your customers to keep returning time and time again. That $4 purchase today might be a $400 purchase next week. It could be thousands during the course of the year.

Find out as much as you can about your customers. Make sure you ask them for e-mail addresses. In fact, have cards ready for them to fill out for "Preferred Customers Sales." For large purchases, send them thank-you notes *by snail mail*. For small purchases, send them e-mail thank-you notes. Send them coupons for discounts on particular items they might be interested in.

In a nutshell . . .

(1) Staying in touch by e-mail is important.
(2) Thank-you notes are important.
(3) An occasional phone call is important.

(4) Flyers announcing upcoming clinics, concerts, and sales events are important.

(5) Getting them to come back one more time is important.

The key here is to stay in touch with your customers. *That's the most important.* Put yourself out there. Let your customers know that you are available anytime for anything regarding the instruments, accessories, and any product information they might need. Make an occasional telephone call, or send a letter that tells customers that you are there to assist. It is important *not* to sell on these occasions. Just let your customers know you are there for them. Come up with your own ways to inform your customers that you are available. Stay in touch. Those "staying in touch" programs can be weeks or months apart. Doing it is most important. How you stay in touch is up to you.

33

Tapping the Adult Market

Letting Your Mature Customers Know the Benefits of Learning to Play

How many times have you heard this: "I have always wanted to play an instrument, but now I'm too old to learn"?

Nonsense. Let your customers know they're never too old to learn, and that studies have shown that learning to play an instrument offers more than just making pleasant sounds. It actually can slow the aging process.

Music helps children with math and reading. Clapping out rhythms connects note values to their numerical equivalents—a half note is twice as long as a quarter note, and its reverse. Rhythm comes naturally to little kids, and besides, it's fun.

Northwestern University conducted a study in which brain response speed was reviewed. Researchers tested young versus old. Half of each age had learned music, half had no music training. The findings offer us well-seasoned brains reason for hope: it appears that music lessons help older folks think faster.

Research focusing on age-related hearing loss extends this theory even further. It looks like learning music could help us hang onto our memories, and even help us hear better when there's lots of noise around us.

"But I didn't study music when I was a kid," you will hear them protest. Bull! Another study at Southern Illinois University's medical school indicates that with older adults, intensive music training can improve speech processing.

Scientific proof is interesting, but the real benefit to making music is simply the making of music. Seniors need to be aware of this, and you simply have to get them in your store.

When they hear one of the old songs from their carefree days, it all comes flooding back. They remember when and where and with whom they were when they used to listen to that song. Often, without really thinking, even the words flow from their throat. Amazing.

Be sure to share this information with your adult customers.

An issue of *Esquire* magazine once stated: "To exercise your brain, learn to play the guitar." Actually any musical instrument will do. So if you're determined to stay sharp, stay active in body and mind. You might not be able to stop the aging process, but you can certainly slow it down. Playing a musical instrument can be just the prescription for a healthier life!

What's nice about mature customers is that they can take lessons anytime during the day (not just after school) and will pay cash for their instrument and anything else you have in the store. They can be encouraged to bring their friends in as well. But here's where it takes a slightly different turn: Teaching adults is not like teaching kids. It has to be fun. They don't want to be talked down to. And if you put them together playing with other people with the same musical ability, you'll have a continual stream of new customers, because they will tell their circle of influence about how much fun they're having and all about their new interest. It's like golf. Few people play golf alone;

they play with three others. Those others are usually their friends, in their same age group and same station in life. Those older people who play golf have no qualms about dropping $500 for a new driver, $60 a dozen for ProV golf balls, or $200 on a new course they never played before. They don't care if they can't break 110; they're having a good time. Maybe they would like to play a guitar, piano, drums, or even a harmonica? Many musical instrument manufacturers are starting to go after this market, as well as some forward-thinking retailers. Everyone else should jump on the bandwagon too, salespeople included.

When you think about your market, don't forget the senior citizens, some of whom have plenty of free time and cash to spend on their music hobbies. Think about ways to invite them and their friends into your store. Some might not relate well to our overpierced and tatted-up staff, but try working around it, and think of ways to reach that market and at least get them in the store.

34

Selling to Senior Customers

There's Gold in the Gray Market

A few years back, I wrote this column in *The Music Trades* magazine. I still believe in every word.

Even though I'm older now, I still frequent music stores quite often. I'm playing more now, even though I'm past 65. I have more free time. I also have more money. I like to stop in to see what's new, and buy stuff like percussion items, keyboard accessories, recording equipment, gifts for friends who play, print music, and many times just an impulsive musical item that I think would be fun to have. I know a lot of people just like me. I have cash. I have disposable income. I sometimes make quick decisions, but for bigger purchases I usually think things through. However, as I get older, there are two things I (and people like me) won't do:

(1) I will not buy from someone I think is a jerk.
(2) I will not buy from someone who doesn't know what they are doing.

Now, having said that, I realize everything is in the mind of the beholder. I know I have some quirks, but a lot of people my age have the same quirkiness. I am not alone. A lot of people my age have the same sentiments. They just don't voice them. They simply don't buy and don't come back.

People in my age group will spend a lot more money with sales-people who we think truly know their business. We buy more from people who like their job, who have some personality, and who make me us feel good. Since I am a serious customer (who just happens to be way past middle age) with serious money to spend, here are a few of my personal likes and dislikes when I come into your store:

(1) I don't want to be called a "senior citizen," "old guy," or "old person." I'll settle for "mature adult" if I have to.
(2) Don't refer to me as "that gray-haired guy." I think my hair is still light brown. I don't remember it changing. Don't remind me.
(3) You don't have to call me "Mr. Popyk" . . . "Bob" is fine with me. I like to buy from people I respect, but I want you to be a friend too.
(4) Don't wear a hat in the store. That shows no respect, and if you have one on I will think you are bald. If it's on backwards I will ask you if you checked the instructions before putting it on.
(5) If I ask you a question, don't read to me from literature or from the side of the box. I can read. My mom taught me when I was 5.
(6) Ask me what type of music I like first. Lady Gaga's latest hit will probably not be my first choice. But it's not going to be Classic '40s either. Let's talk.
(7) If the T-shirt you're wearing has a creative use of the "F" word, I will probably not buy from you.
(8) If your tattoos and body piercings are taken to a new level, you will probably gross me out and I will look for another

salesperson. I will also wonder what the loan officer at your
bank will think when you come in for a mortgage or a loan.
But, hey, that's my generation.

(9) Have a good attitude. Attitude is everything. Be your best at all
times. Don't tell me you'd rather be out playing, or working
someplace else. Believe in yourself and your store.

(10) This is important—very important. Ask me some engaging
questions. Talk to me. Try to get to know me a little bit. Don't
use stupid closes on me. Just look for a need and try to fill it.
Be nice. Ask me to buy.

Now if you have taken offense to any of this, I am sorry. However,
I also don't care. The nicest part of being older with more time and
more money is that we can buy where and when we want. Don't think
for a minute we are in the minority. People in our age bracket are living longer than ever before. Our segment of the buying population
is larger than ever.

Here are a couple of secrets on selling us "old timers" (call us that
and we will probably whack you on the side of your head with the
nearest music stand). First, "give without the expectation of getting."
Don't try to "sell" us. Just help us buy. This is the hardest thing for a
salesperson to do with older people, but it's an important key to getting high-level acceptance with mature adults. We know the tricks
and the BS. Save it for the less-savvy younger customers. Be genuine.
Remember, "the more you give, the more you get."

Secondly, position yourself as a resource. When you give us value
with your knowledge and expertise, and you can provide information beyond what your store or instrument manufacturers provide,
you will be recommended, sought after, referred, and highly spoken
about, to all of the other people we know. We talk. We have friends
our age. If you understand us, we will get you more customers than
you can imagine. If we like you, we will tell everyone we know. If we
don't, we will tell even more.

35

How Important Are Your Business Cards?

Business cards are both the wave of the future and the way of the past. The cards may be low tech, but they can leave an indelible impression. Think of the Lone Ranger. With a flurry of hoofs, a cloud of dust, and a hearty "Hi-yo, Silver," the Lone Ranger rides off into the sunset leaving everyone saying, "Who was that masked man?" And what did he leave behind for the people to remember him by? A shotgun shell? A spent .22 caliber cartridge? No. A silver bullet! Something that set him apart from all the rest. So you've got two choices when handing out your business card. You can hand out a silver bullet in a memorable way, or you can just take a spent shell out of your pocket and hope for the best.

A business card is your signature. It reveals a lot about you. The Lone Ranger didn't carry his silver bullets around in his pocket, getting dirty, scratched, and dusty. He kept them in his ammo belt so they always looked brand new. And he always presented silver bullets in a way that made recipients proud to accept them. They didn't throw them out. They kept them around. They couldn't wait to show them to their friends.

You, however, don't want to leave potential customers saying, "Who was that masked man?" Make sure they know. Make sure they remember. Make sure they know who you are and what you do. Most importantly, leave an impression so ingrained that they automatically keep you in mind for the future. However, you need more than a good-looking card to help create more business for you.

What's more important is the person behind the card. A jerk with a great-looking business card is still a jerk. You need a little personality along with personal contact. You need to work on your schmoozing skills, and you need to capitalize on your own "magic circle" of influence. The more people you talk to, the better your chance of doing more business. Business cards are an integral part of networking.

When someone asks what you do, you have been given the perfect opportunity to give out a business card. Explain what you do as you hand over your card. Do you have a unique answer when someone asks what you do? What do you say when you hand out your business card? Come up with something that fits your personality, something that can make an impression. Then all you have to do is start finding more people you can give your card to.

Maybe the next person doesn't necessarily need a musical instrument. Maybe she is not quite interested in the music business. But once you establish a little rapport, get her to be your friend, *and after you find out what she does,* you might just say, "If you were to go into my business tomorrow, with whom would you talk?"

And most times you will get a name. It will probably be to get you off her back. But hey, you might just get a great lead. A super contact. Someone else to give your business card to. And it goes on from there.

Here are some basics for handing out business cards and getting a response:

(1) Have them with you at all times.
(2) Don't hand over the card as soon as it is requested. Talk a little first.
(3) Don't hand over the card and shake hands at the same time. Do one at a time.

(4) Give a genuine handshake and smile.

(5) Remember the name of the person you are talking to.

(6) Say something that clever that will be like a 10-second commercial for you and your business.

(7) Don't be afraid to give out two cards and ask for a referral.

(8) Humble yourself.

(9) Don't give out a dirty, soiled card. Better make no impression than a bad impression.

(10) Keep track of whom you give cards to. Develop a system of remembering which contacts are the most important.

(11) Contact these people at a later date; use their names and mention that you would like a chance to speak to them again about something you forgot to mention.

Put one in every bag and with every instrument, and ask that customers refer you to their friends, neighbors, acquaintances, and people they meet on the street who might be interested in a musical instrument.

Everyone should have his or her own business cards. Come up with funny titles if you cater to a hipper market. And don't just give your staff the cards. Explain how to get them out there.

36

Referral Selling

It is common sense to make the most out of a satisfied customer. Customers like to let people know what astute buyers they are. They like to spread the wealth. If they're happy, they tell other people. If they aren't, you've got a real problem.

As mentioned earlier, calling the customer after the sale to ensure satisfaction can be very important, plus it can lead to more business. Here's the perfect moment to ask for a referral. Who else do they know? Who do they know who also might be interested in a new instrument?

When salespeople (who didn't call customers after a sale to see if everything was okay) were interviewed, they said things like, "I didn't want to hear about any problems," or "What if they had second thoughts?" or "What if they thought they paid too much?" Guess what. You can't afford to have even one unhappy customer. One disgruntled customer will tell 20 friends. If you can make that customer happy, he might tell the same people a different story. That brings in more business.

If you ask customers to buy and then they sign on the dotted line, that's great. And if you've got their trust, that's even better. If you make sure they're happy and they refer you to their friends as well, you'll never have to worry about where your next sale is coming from.

Sometimes it doesn't take a lot to jumpstart your sales force. Sometimes it just takes a little creativity and common sense.

So *ask for a referral.*

Getting referrals is an incredibly effective technique for creating a steady stream of prospects and new customers. Here's why referral-generated customers are so important:

(1) Referral customers are the most cost-efficient, profitable, and loyal source of new business you could ever hope to have.

(2) Referral customers are quicker to buy, more reliable, less price resistant, and an outstanding source of more referrals!

And getting great referrals is easy; all you really have to do is ask!

Many of our clients tell us that "word of mouth" already brings a steady stream of new customers—but that they don't do much to actively solicit that new business.

Just imagine what an incredibly powerful source of new customers a systematic method of asking for referrals and testimonials would be!

You have to ask, not just hope, for referrals.

The easiest referral system is this: every employee hands his or her customer two business cards at the end of the sale and asks, "Would you do me a favor? If you had a good time here and enjoy the new guitar, will you please tell a couple of friends? Thanks!" Simple and effective.

Who else do you know? Ask them if they would tell their friends about your store and maybe suggest they come in, to see you personally. One happy customer will tell 10 others, and out of that 10 a few might come in . . . if you ask.

37

Selling Lesson Programs

Lessons are a commodity within themselves. They bring people in the store every week. Don't forget to mention your lesson programs to every customer who comes in. They might not need lessons for themselves, but they could have family, friends, or acquaintances who might want to learn to play. Lessons sell instruments, so you want to get your name out there as the place to come to learn how to play the instruments of their choice.

Here are 15 ideas to market and promote your music studios and the teachers in your store:

(1) **Use your local schools.** Put a small advertisement in a school newsletter—many schools run a newsletter on a monthly basis that is given to all the families of the school. If you placed a small ad in one and ran an offer of a free lesson or something to prompt people to call, it would cost a lot less than putting one in a bigger newspaper publication, and you could easily target the clients you really want.

(2) **Offer a free trial lesson.** This is great for getting parents and children inspired in playing. They get to know you, you get to

talk about your teachers and your store, and you can start a strong relationship right from the beginning.

(3) **Offer a free workshop or performance to a local school or civic group**. Just playing in front of people inspires us to play. Be seen and heard.

(4) **Have a pamphlet or flyer promoting your lesson programs.** Print materials require a little setup money, but they let people know where you are and what you do. It's amazing how long they can be kept on a refrigerator, especially if they have a free offer in them somewhere.

(5) **Organize a "come and try session" during the holidays.** Give people something to do during the holidays, and offer a free group or single lesson to increase their interest in music.

(6) **Implement a referral program.** If customers tell friends to come and sign up with one of your teachers, give them a gift and/or a free lesson or two to show them that you value their business.

(7) **Make your studio comfortable for students and parents to wait in.** Parents spend a lot of time in your music studio, so make it comfortable, and they'll want to be there more and will want to tell their friends about you. You could include a coffee machine, magazines, or things for children to do while they are waiting. It's amazing the value this adds to your business.

(8) **Place a small ad offering a free music lesson in your local pennysaver.** (See chapter 29.)

(9) **Have your teachers offer their services as a player or accompanist to a local club, church, school or other organization on a voluntary basis.** This will give them the opportunity to promote themselves and your store at the same time.

(10) **Place cards and flyers on local community bulletin boards.** You just need to search them out.

(11) **Give your students small logo gifts.** You can get imprinted music pencils, pens, magnets and other items that identify you and your store. You'll be amazed at where these things end up and who they are given to!

(12) **Keep in communication with the parents of your students.** It costs you nothing, and you can really help them by giving them information on special offers they might want to know about or upcoming concert events.

(13) **Host a concert or recital for your students, and let them invite friends and family members.** Recitals work! Book a hall (if your store isn't big enough), and let your students be the stars of the show. You can also use this as a chance to put a flyer or pamphlet on each chair offering a free lesson or asking people to come see you at the store for some free information or something else that may be of value.

(14) **Host a parent night.** Parents love to come into your studio or school and talk about and see pictures of their children, talk to other parents, and hear about the benefits of music for their children. Wrap up the evening with a door prize. Parents will talk about your philosophies to other parents and become raving fans of what you do.

(15) **Make your music lessons *fun*.** Students who are having fun will tell other students, and students who are having fun will have happy parents, who will tell other parents and their kids.

38

Selling Through Your Lesson Studios

Your lesson programs can create musicians of all ages, as well as loyal customers who buy for these students. But have you considered that your program can also attract new customers in the community when you schedule in-store events? Build excitement for music making, including student performances, quarterly recitals, holiday performances, "battle of the bands" contests, jam sessions, and drum circles! In addition, your music teachers can lead clinics, minilessons, and master classes for the community. The more you show people *how* to play, the more likely they are to consider getting lessons and/or gear. Promote your lessons and in-store events by utilizing your website with teacher bios, student testimonials, and a forum to discuss your store's program—the events that students get to do beyond lessons. By establishing your store as a destination for lesson programs and performances, you can create excitement in your community for those who want to listen and learn to play themselves.

A few things you might want to remember: Make sure every student (and particularly his or her parent) is acknowledged when coming in. If it is an adult student, this is critically important. Have pictures of the current instruments and gear in every studio. Make sure the instruments are of the same quality or even better than what the student has at home. Urge students to try out better instruments. Kids will tell their parents how great the instruments were at your store. Maybe the parents will talk to you about getting their children new instruments as they get better, or as gifts along the way. Suggest to parents an upgrade for current instruments as the weeks go by.

Have a photo gallery. Keep pictures of all your students on a wall in your lesson area. Let customers know you have a great clientele for music lessons and teaching to play is not something you do as an afterthought. You want to generate traffic every day in your music store, and music lessons are the way to do it.

Have a meeting with your staff on their ideas for generating more music students. Update your print material with pictures of your teachers, and scheduled events. Make sure you list all of the instruments that are taught in your store. Have everyone on your staff promote your music studios every day of the year. Lessons are not only a revenue source; they are a way to really increase your instrument sales.

39

Keep Individual Customer Lists

It's important that all salespeople have their own customer lists. This includes the people they've sold to, their leads, the people they have talked to on the phone, and the people who regularly text them, e-mail them, or stay in contact with them in some way.

This is invaluable for day-to-day business when your store is having a major promotion. When you print up flyers, have your salespeople mail them with personal notes to the customers on their lists.

Also, when you send out an e-mail blast, include personal notes (attached in the e-mail) from your sales staff, using their lists.

When business slows down and no one is coming in the door, you can ask your salespeople to call a couple of people on their customer lists and try to get them in to evaluate a new instrument, give their opinions on a recent trade, or just chat about who they might know that would be interested in any type of higher-priced musical instrument. This is why it's extremely valuable to have individual customer lists.

Think about forming an advisory committee for your store with your sales team's best customers. Get them mugs or T-shirts that say, "[Your Store] Advisory Committee." Call them when a new instrument comes in. Get their feedback. If they have no interest in participating themselves, ask who they know that might be interested. They're part of your store at this point. Hopefully they will be part of your fan base too.

40

Learning About Your Customers

Here's some Marketing 101 (the stuff we say we know and then don't pay attention to):

(1) Know who your best customers are . . . those who frequently spend time in your store and are easy to do business with.
(2) Find out what type of music they like to play or listen to.
(3) Get to know who their friends and relatives are who play or have an interest in music.
(4) Know which medium or media they respond to.
(5) Find out what it will take to get them in the store on a regular basis.
(6) Know how your salespeople stay in touch with these people (if they do at all) and the follow-up and the sales.

It has been said that business success is 85 percent people skills and 15 percent product knowledge. In selling musical instruments, this may be more heavily skewed toward those interpersonal skills. When you ask music salespeople if they feel it is important to develop relationships with their customers, they invariably say yes. But when you ask them how they do this, they don't seem to know what to say. It seems that many people struggle with how to develop those crucial business relationships.

Until you know who your customers are and what they like (and act on this information in a way that demonstrates that you care), you are not going to progress in your relationship with those individuals. Most of us tend to be "me-focused" and enjoy talking about ourselves—and this applies to our customers. Therefore, it helps to learn about your customers. Find out what they are truly interested in and get excited about.

Oftentimes salespeople do not know where to start in order to learn about their customers. It helps to be able to have a guide to what type of information you should be gathering.

Find out about their families. Ask questions about parents, children, or siblings, particularly who else plays, what other instruments they have in their home, and other musical interests. Ask about their occupations or what they do, what they would like to do, what they are studying, or what they like best about their jobs. Talk about recreational interests or ask questions about what they like to do during their spare time besides music. Find out what motivates them in life.

Keeping these questions in mind will help you think of other questions to ask your customers so you can develop an understanding of them. And knowing more about them as individuals and caring about them is a great first step. Taking a few minutes to learn more about your customers will help you develop deeper relationships with them. Odds are you'll see the results reflected not only in how your customers respond to you but also in your sales numbers.

41

What Problems Are We Facing?

Do you involve your staff in any of your day-to-day store challenges? Do they know about problems you might have with suppliers? Are they aware of your weekly expenses? Do they know what you are trying to do to promote business and get more people in the door? Are they aware of any customer complaints and how you attempt to resolve them? Are they aware of any new financing options for customers?

It might be a good idea to sit down with your staff once or twice a month and get some feedback on ways to improve your operation. Maybe there won't be many good ideas (and some might be a little off the wall), but at least their voices will be heard. Maybe there are negative online comments you aren't aware of. Maybe there are returns you don't know about. Maybe your competition is involved in areas you are unfamiliar with.

Ask questions. Find out what's on your employees' minds. Here are a few things you might want to ask them directly:

(1) What problems do we have that I might not be aware of?
(2) What ways can we make our store better?

(3) Have we had any negative comments from customers?

(4) Are customers asking for anything we don't stock?

(5) Have there been any objections from customers that we haven't been able to handle?

(6) Are our phones being handled correctly?

(7) Do we have any problems with any of our teachers?

(8) Are there any sales being lost that we should have made?

(9) Can you see opportunities we might be aware of in any of our departments?

Make your own list. Ask your employees to make theirs. You know most of the problems you're facing on a day-to-day basis, but maybe there are a few you don't know exist. Look at some of them from the eyes of your staff. Get their input. They'll feel they're an important part of your operation, and you'll be all the better for it.

42

Handling Complaints and Dissatisfied Customers

As mentioned previously (and reiterated here for importance), study after study has shown that 1 dissatisfied customer will tell at least 20 other people of his or her negative experience. Simple mathematics says if 3 customers leave your store dissatisfied in some way or other every day, they will tell of their experiences to a total of 60 other people.

That means that over a one-year period, some 22,000 potential customers could possibly have a negative impression of your store. Can anyone afford to let this happen? No! It's a very competitive world out there, and the pressure is increasing all of the time. Making dissatisfied customers satisfied is one of the keys to surviving and thriving in this environment.

Most salespeople in music stores deal with many challenging customer situations. These situations may include:

(1) A customer who is upset about the quality of an instrument.
(2) An instrument return or a cancellation order.
(3) Incorrect information given to the customer.
(4) A customer who is negative toward your music store due to
      past experiences.

(5) A confrontational issue or conflict.

(6) Explaining a company policy or procedure.

The ultimate goal in these challenging situations is to provide a win-win solution. We want our customer to leave the interaction feeling listened to, well taken care of, and valued. A customer-focused mindset will have a tremendous impact on accomplishing these goals. Along with customer focus, an invaluable tool for dealing with challenging situations is the following five-step process.

Think about this: Have you ever been an upset customer, calling your product or service provider with a serious problem? If you receive a satisfactory resolution *and* you feel listened to, well taken care of, and valued during your interaction, aren't you likely to consider doing business with this company again? This five-step process will help you provide your customers with this positive experience. Aside from reaching a win-win solution, the goal of the five-step process is to leave your customers feeling listened to, well taken care of, and valued. Let's examine the specific steps.

Step 1—Strategize: How Do You Develop a Strategy?

(1) Develop your goal for the interaction. What do you want as the end result—for example, keep the customer, resolve an issue, and so forth?

(2) Identify your parameters. What can you do or provide the customer independently? What *can't* you do because of policy or business reasons?

(3) Prepare by identifying common problems and win-win solutions.

Your strategy should be to arrive at a solution that will be a win for both your music store and the customer. If you are successful, you will retain the customer, exceed his or her expectations, and provide a very positive experience so that he or she will want to continue doing business with your store.

Step 2—Acknowledge

The acknowledgement is essential to communicating in challenging situations. Use phrases like, "I understand how you feel," "I apologize," and "I can see how you might feel that way," so that customers feel that they have been heard and that you respect them. It clears the way for you to move forward by helping diffuse the emotion and placing you on the side of the customer.

Step 3—Clarify

Sometimes we mistakenly proceed to resolve a problem based on what we *think* the customer was saying. This third step of the process allows you to clarify and draw out information to make sure that you understand the customer's true concern. Examples of clarifying might include:

(1) "What I hear you saying is _____; is that right?"
(2) "Can you tell me more about _____?"
(3) "How may I help you _____?"
(4) "What were you hoping would happen when _____?"

Clarifying leads you to the appropriate solution in a more efficient manner.

Step 4—Present Resolution

The fourth step is to present a resolution. Presenting a resolution should not be a challenge if you've done the first three steps properly.

As you present the resolution, you want to state specifically what you are going to do for the customer. You may also offer alternatives. It is critical to understand your parameters—what you *can* do for the customer and what you *can't* do.

Step 5—Check-Back

The check-back is your opportunity to make sure that the customer is satisfied and feels good about the resolution. Examples of check-backs include:

(1) "How does that sound?"
(2) "What do you think about _____?"
(3) "Are you with me?"
(4) "Does that make sense?"
(5) "Will that meet your needs?"
(6) "Would that be satisfactory?"

Above all, don't let your customer walk out the store with you feeling "I showed them" and the customer feeling "I'll never come back here again." Try to make every dissatisfied customer feel some sort of satisfaction.

43

Getting Your Salespeople Involved in Niche Markets

Do you have a specific niche in your music business? Are you a full-line music store that caters to anyone looking for any type of musical instrument and is competing with similar music stores and everyone on the Internet, or are you a music store specializing in a more selective inventory of products?

The way you go about building your music business differs according to whether you are a broad-niche marketer or a narrow-niche specialist. Both have their advantages.

Stores that stock with a broad inventory of musical instruments gather a lot of attention from a broad spectrum of people. However, there are also a lot of dealers in those "broad niches," and it can be hard to stand out from the crowd and get people's attention. Narrower niches get attention from people who are looking for a specific type of musical instrument. There are fewer prospective customers in narrow niches, but they are often eager buyers. Not only that; customers love talking about the instruments and will often pay more just to have a friend (that's you) whose interests are the same.

Ask your salespeople where their musical interests lie. (You might be surprised.)

There are many musical instruments today that appealed to mass markets years ago and are now considered niche markets. Think about it. In the '40s and '50s, there was a huge accordion industry. There were accordion studios, accordion bands, and many, many different makes of accordions. Now it's a niche business, yet many accordion dealers (or music stores with accordion departments) survive today and still make decent money. There are only a few, but they're out there. Button boxes are big for Cajun and Tex-Mex markets, yet many music stores have none of these accordions in stock. The polka thing never went away, and accordions are still a major part of that sound, yet you don't see them lining the shelves of most music stores. Did you know more accordions are sold than home organs today? Uh oh . . . home organs, the high-profit, big-hit musical instrument of the '60s and '70s. That business is now a shell of its former self, yet there are dealers who still make a serious living in just selling home organs while everyone else turns down their noses at them. The list of niche-market musical products goes on and on.

Do your salespeople have some unique musical interests?

Steel drums, gongs, Caribbean instruments, Irish instruments such as bodhrans (or any type of ethic instrument), and *pianos* are all considered niche markets. Who would have ever thought the piano business would be a niche market? Fifty years ago, pianos dominated the NAMM trade shows. Now the American manufacturers are next to none, and acoustic pianos are no longer the staple in homes they once were. There used to be more piano stores in some towns than pizza shops. Now in some cities, it's tough to find even one piano dealer. But believe it or not, people still buy acoustic pianos, and the margin is pretty darn good. How about this: There is a music store in a town of 26,000 people that specializes in phonograph needles. The owner knows phonographs inside out. People come in for needles, like to talk about things like the antique phonograph they inherited from their grandparents, and end up buying other instruments the store offers. That's not to mention the very high markup on the needles themselves.

Niche musical product marketing can be extremely cost effective. For instance, imagine you offer musical instruments that are just right for a select demographic or ethnic group in your area, such as Hispanics or Asians. You could advertise on ethnic radio stations, which have considerably lower rates than stations that program for broader audiences. So your marketing budget would go a lot further, allowing you to advertise with greater frequency or use a more comprehensive media mix.

If you are going to specialize in any type of niche musical instrument, it's imperative to speak your customers' language. In other words, you should understand that instrument market's "hot buttons" and be prepared to communicate with those people as an understanding member of the group—not an outsider.

Here's the process to finding niche musical instruments that can make money for you:

(1) Find a niche instrument you and your salespeople are passionate about. This will greatly improve your chances of being successful, because it's the only way you're going to be able to devote the time and effort to create a meaningful website, build up the right traffic, generate worthwhile income, and enjoy what you're doing.

(2) Choose a niche instrument you are knowledgeable about. If you don't have the knowledge yet, then choose a niche instrument that you would love to promote, and then spend the necessary time to research it, so you can eventually become an expert in your specialized instrument niche.

(3) Define your niche market. Do the necessary research to actually see if there is a market for the niche instrument you might want to specialize in.

Niche musical instruments might be low volume, but they can be high margin if promoted and marketed correctly. Check out other music stores in your area. Is there something they are not carrying that you can specialize in? You might be surprised. The ideas are endless.

44

Keep It Clean

Have you ever gone into a store to buy something, and the item was dusty? Doesn't really make you want to pay the full price, does it? Or have you ever gone into a small shop where the salesperson is eating lunch at his desk, and the whole place smells like McDonald's? It's just not the right atmosphere for spending a lot of money. If you are a small to mid-sized music store competing with much larger competition, don't let anyone get the best of you in the cleanliness department. Maybe your music store is a fraction of the size of the store down the street, but there's no reason it shouldn't be equally clean, or cleaner. In fact, you may be losing sales—right now—because your business looks sloppier than you realize. Now before you just say, "Not me" and turn the page, take a look at your store from the eyes of your customers. Here's a little 10-point check list. How do you stack up?

(1) **Handwritten Signs:** No matter what they say, the real message is you cut corners. What's more, "temporary" signs often become permanent eyesores.
(2) **Dusty Lights, Fixtures, Instruments:** Film and dust on light bulbs, fixtures, and stock make your place look dingy. Wash,

dust, and vacuum regularly. Don't let your instruments look like they've been there a long time. Dust raises doubts about the quality of the merchandise.

(3) **Clutter:** Maybe you lack storage space, but keep your place tidy. Don't let paper accumulate on desks and in corners. Get rid of yesterday's coffee cups. Make sure the instruments are all in their proper places when you leave the store, and are easy to find and try out the next day. Each day you want to start with a clean slate and a new attitude.

(4) **Odors:** Unpleasant odors can build up gradually so you don't notice them, but customers will. Constantly police your store for any trouble areas. Adding flowers and automatic odor neutralizer dispensers can help.

(5) **Worn-Out Paint:** Walls and doors endure an unavoidable pounding. Schedule regular touch-ups. Save the extra paint for future needs whenever you have painting done.

(6) **Dirty Bathrooms:** Do you let customers use them? Would Snow White want to use your bathrooms? They should be clean and pristine and give a good impression of your entire store.

(7) **Dirty and Unorganized Stock Arrangement:** If you're a small music store and see a lot of the same customers regularly, it's important that you rotate your instruments and keep displays fresh. Find your store's hot spot and keep new instruments in that area to maintain better margins.

(8) **Dingy Fluorescents:** Does your floor look spectacular or subdued? Are you catching your customer's eye with overheads and other lighting technique to make your instruments sparkle? Fluorescents are not enough.

(9) **Unprofessional Price Tags:** Is everything marked? The big guys have tags on everything. The other retailers do too. Customers are starting to be suspicious of anything where they have to ask the price. If you are discounting or putting

something on sale, put "was" and "is" if you have to, but make sure everything is tagged.

(10) **Taped-Up Point-of-Sale (and Other) Signs:** You want to let instruments help sell themselves by using signs that explain features and benefits, but don't have something up so long the tape yellows. I can't tell you the number of stores where I've seen this. Clever POS signs are good for smaller (and even larger) music stores. Browsers and others who prefer not to talk to sales staffers will learn about the instrument while you focus on customers who want personal attention. But don't have the same ones up all the time. And that goes for other signs too. Maybe you made the newspapers for community services five years ago, and the paper is still taped to the wall. Yellow tape, yellow paper. If something is that important, frame it.

No one runs a dirty-looking business intentionally—it creeps in unnoticed. Music stores start out clean and sharp, and then little things happen. One here, two there. You may not notice them because you are always there, but they add up and turn off prospects that walk into your place cold. Appearance is a quick way for a customer to assess your competence. Cleanliness inspires confidence.

45

Separating Yourself from the Pack

You're an expert in the music business. You have your own store(s), probably can play, know features and benefits like there's no tomorrow, and are a master at demonstrating anything on your floor. If you're not closing as many sales as you'd like, it probably has nothing to do with your ability to talk about your musical instruments. It could, however, have everything to do with your ability to talk about yourself.

It doesn't matter how good you are if you're the only one who knows it. Maybe now's the time to take a step up on your soapbox and let more of the world know you exist. Think about this for a minute: How do you differentiate yourself from your competition? What makes you and your music store so special? Do you have a personal 30-second commercial about your business that sets you apart from everybody else? Well, with business getting tight and the economy in the dump, you really should take a good look at why you and your store stand out from all the rest.

When someone asks, "Why should I buy from you?" (as opposed to the store down the street, the catalogues, or the Internet), does your response sound like one of the following?

(1) "We've been in business for over 10 years."
(2) "We've got great service."
(3) "We've got great quality."
(4) "We've got better prices than anybody else around."
(5) "We stand behind every sale."

Big deal. Your local car dealer, dry cleaner, or appliance store probably says the same think. How are you so different? Let's start with your after-hours answering machine or voice mail. Does your message say, "We're not here to take your call right now; please leave your name, phone number, and message, and we'll call you back"? Well, so does everybody else's. You're missing a great opportunity to insert your own personal commercial in a voice-mail message with one great, important, terrific word . . . *only*. That's it. It can be that simple. Would you rather go to a heart specialist who has been practicing for more than 10 years, or one who "is the only doctor to be acknowledged by the Harvard Medical Research Institute as a leading area practitioner?" Which is more attention getting: an answering machine message that simply asks for a name and phone number or one that lets the caller know that you are "the only store that's open seven days a week including evenings," or "the area's only music store with a full staff of teachers for all instruments including keyboard, strings, wind instruments, drums, and guitar"? Are you the only music store owner who plays professionally in a rock band/symphony/string quartet/jazz group as well? Are you the only music store to receive a special award? Are you the only Yamaha, Steinway, Fender, Gibson, Peavey, Roland, or Martin dealer for miles around? Are you the only salesperson to receive accreditation of accomplishment from a specific manufacturer?

You can have a lot of "onlys." But if you don't bring them up, no one will ever know. So practice that 30-second elevator speech. Come up with your own short commercial about yourself. Practice until you can recite it without even thinking. This way, when someone at a cocktail party asks what you do, you can spontaneously say, "I sell musical

instruments at Acme Music World. We're the only _____."
Or: "I own Hometown Music Center. We're the only _____
and we specialize in _____." What a difference.

To stand out from the crowd, you have to be unique. To be unique, you have to be the only one of your kind. Do a little soul searching, and figure out what keeps you from being a carbon copy of other music stores or salespeople in town. Do a little survey of your customers, and ask why they bought from you. You might be surprised. It could be you were the only store that was open on Sunday. You were the only store that taught banjo or violin. Maybe you were the only store endorsed by a well-known rock group. Or maybe you were the only sales team that knew the intricacies of a particular instrument. Maybe you were the only store that carried a full line of Latin percussion instruments. Or you were the only store that offered 60-month financing. Maybe you were the only salesperson to come to someone's home to assess a trade, offered delivery, or had a spot where small children could be entertained while parents made a purchase.

Sift through all those "onlys" and find the one that sets you apart from all the other music stores. Then capitalize on it. People do business with people they like, and people tend to like the unique, stand-out-from-the-rest type of store or person. If people like you, they'll trust you. If they trust you, they'll be more inclined to buy from you. Your "only" can make all the difference.

46

Try to Look Happy (Even If You Are Not)

Not all days can be good days. Don't take it out on your customer or let it show on your face.

Bad days happen to the best of us—days when you just wake up in a really bad mood. Days when something (or nothing) has made you angry, sad, frustrated, disappointed—whatever. Days where you know up front that "man, this is going to suck."

You still have to get up and go to work, but before you even get there, you're already seething inside. You try to do your job, but somehow all of the angry, dissatisfied penny-pinching, pain-in-the-neck customers have come in on the same day.

Everything your coworkers say to you sounds incredibly stupid. Everyone seems out to annoy you. The next person to open his mouth is likely to get his head ripped clean off.

Not much fun, huh? Luckily, you can do something about it. Here are six ways to turn around a bad day.

(1) **Accept your bad mood.** Being in a bad mood is not that difficult to do. Being in a bad mood while trying to force yourself to cheer up really sucks. Fighting a bad mood only

prolongs it, so if you're mad, be mad. If you're sad, be sad. This does not give you license to be rude and unpleasant to innocent bystanders. It just means that you need to recognize and accept your bad mood to be able to do something about it.

(2) **Tell others.** You can try to keep you bad mood a secret and put on your happy mask. Guess what, you're fooling nobody. Your coworkers will notice and they will wonder what they've done to piss you off. The best thing to do is to tell the people you work closely with. Simply tell them, "Listen, guys, I'm in a really sour mood today. I'm not sure why, but it's nothing you have done. If I bite your head off, I apologize in advance."

(3) **Look inside first.** Truly successful people are not the smart ones but the ones with the best emotional skills.

You need to have these two skills:

(1) The ability to identify and name your emotional states and to understand the link between emotions, thought, and action.

(2) The capacity to manage your emotional states—to control emotions or to shift undesirable emotional states to more acceptable ones.

In other words, you need to rely on your ability to recognize and deal with your own emotions.

We tend to think that a bad mood is always caused by something or someone else. And when we're in a bad mood, everything suddenly becomes annoying, making it even easier to find justifications for the bad mood.

But not every bad mood has a reason. Maybe you just slept badly. Or you're coming down with the flu. Or you're just having a bad day.

Instead, you must look inside yourself first, to see what might or might not be the cause of your negative emotional state. Here's one way to do it.

(1) Remember the good stuff. When you're in a foul mood, everything is bad. But the good things you appreciated yesterday, where you weren't as annoyed, are probably still there—you're just not seeing them. Spend a few moments to try think of at least one or two things that aren't all bad. Something you look forward to. A person you like at work. Something nice that happened recently.

(2) This too shall pass. You've been in a bad mood before. It passed. So will this one. It's no big deal.

(3) Take some quiet time. And if you're having a really bad day, it may be a good idea to withdraw a little if you can. Take a walk during your lunch break. Sit and work somewhere quiet. Nothing lasts forever. You'll be in a good mood again before you know it.

47

Attitude

This is probably the most obvious method to any good customer service experience, and like most good ideas, untrained sales associates usually abandon it. Your attitude will immediately determine whether or not customers are even going to give you the *chance* to change their minds. If you treat them like intrusions on your day, they will sense it immediately.

Attitude is everything. If you don't like what you are doing, update your résumé. It's time for a career change. You are what you believe.

The music business is a business where customers come in on many occasions to make major purchases. Money can be an issue, but more often than not, it is not the main issue. People buy from salespeople they can trust. They buy from salespeople who know their products inside and out. And they buy from salespeople who really love the business they're in. They go out of their way to avoid salespeople who complain about their jobs, dislike their stores, hate their employers, or have the weight of the world on their shoulders. And they hate to deal with salespeople who are continually having a bad day.

Do a quick attitude check. What's your "smile frequency"? Do you really like your job? Would you rather be in another line of work?

When you wake up in the morning, are you really anxious to get to the store, or would you rather be playing a gig or maybe not in sales at all? When a customer tells you that she can buy a similar instrument cheaper down the street or online, how do you react? Do you start to simmer inside? And when you lose a sale to a competitor, do you take it out on your next customer who's looking for a lower price? Do you carry any personal problems from home into your store?

When business slows down, when your competition is giving the stuff away, when customers start asking for lines you don't carry, when nasty customers start making you their entertainment for the day, how do you react? Do you lash back, sneer, snarl, and wish you were doing something else? Or do you hang in there with a good attitude, knowing things will be better?

Abraham Lincoln once said, "It's not what happens to you, it's how you handle what happens to you that determines your happiness in life." Life is too short to have to deal with a bad attitude. Particularly when it's someone else's. A good attitude will help bring customers back, one more time. With a bad attitude, you may never see them again.

In the music business, the dealers with the best attitudes are going to prevail. Forget the moaning and whining, just decide to do something positive about it. America saw it after the Great Depression. We saw it after the economic consumer crisis of the late '70s, and we are seeing it now. Attitude is going to make the difference, so let me give you a few attitude-adjustment quotes from Mark Twain, Joe Calloway, Sun Tzu, and my cousin Nonin who is a Buddhist monk in Omaha, NE.

Copy the one (or ones) you like the best, and put them on your phone or on your wall where you can see them every day:

Many struggling stores have everything they need to succeed. The pieces just aren't in alignment.

There are a lot of stores that can compete and win in markets that no longer exist.

What do you need to let go of? Can you do it today?

You can't get what you want until you make the space. What do you need to change so that opportunity can open up?

If you are afraid to fail, you won't get what you want.

Bravery is not the absence of fear, but the master of fear.

If you are successful, that means you know what used to work.

You don't build a brand with advertising. You build a brand with consistency of performance.

Is what I'm doing right now making me any money or helping my business?

And my favorite:

There has never been a moment when you do not have the power to alter your destiny.

When the housing prices come back, gas prices are no longer in crisis mode, and the stock market regains its strength, people will still be making music and hoping to own the stuff our industry offers. Just get ready, it's going to happen. If you think it won't get any better or if you think it will get worse, you will become the prophet of your own destiny. If you think you're going to succeed, you will. So be careful in your beliefs. Your customers can tell if you believe in yourself of not. Success breeds success. Customers are going to shop in stores that look successful, and look they are going to be around for years to come. They did in the past, and they are doing it today. Everyone loves a winner, and being a winner starts by looking like one.

48

Believe in Your Store

Your customers can choose to shop at many different places: other brick-and-mortar stores, catalogs, TV shopping channels, the Internet, warehouse clubs, and more.

Why do your customers decide to stop shopping at your store and try out one of the competition? You might guess price, convenience, selection, or service to be at the top of the list, but you'd guess wrong. Market surveys tell us that . . .

67 percent of customers stop shopping with you because of perceived indifference.

Plain and simple, they think you don't care about them. They think you don't care if they shop with you or not. If most people stop shopping with you because they think you don't care, logic dictates that by showing that you *do* care, you can *keep* them as customers for life. Smile, look them in the eye, and give a warm, genuine, "Thanks for shopping with us. We hope to see you again soon" at the end of each sale. If it comes from the heart, it never fails to impress.

Marketing genius Jay Abraham puts it this way: "The secret to success is to fall out of love with your product, service, or store, and fall in love with your customers."

When you make "The Big Switch," all of your business decisions suddenly revolve around what's best for your customers, not what's most convenient for you.

(1) Your language will suit your customers' preferences and styles, not your own.
(2) Your product assortment will reflect what your customers like, not what you like.
(3) Your store policies will be written with your customers' best interests in mind.
(4) Your store hours will fit your customers' schedules, not yours.
(5) Your return policies will be generous and not restrictive.
(6) Your staff will be thoroughly trained so your customers get the same great service from everyone in your business that they get from you.

Be proud of your store and being able to serve the musical-instrument-buying public. Too often, people here in America feel that working to serve others is not a job to be proud of. That serving makes them somehow inferior to the person on the other side of the cash register, desk, or table. And those feelings show up in job performance as unwillingness, rudeness, or simply indifference. Feeling pride in your company, your work, and your ability to truly serve others comes through loud and clear in job performance too. It shows up as fun and friendliness, as the desire to please each customer (especially the tough ones!), as the thoughtful extras, no matter how small, that make each transaction special. It shows up as innovative ideas and creative solutions to problems.

49

Believe in the Benefits of Music

Music delivers benefits for young and old alike, and you need to believe that in order to be successful in the music business.

Here are ten benefits of a musical education (share them with your customers):

(1) Early musical training helps develop brain areas involved in language and reasoning. It is thought that brain development continues for many years after birth. Recent studies have clearly indicated that musical training physically develops the part of the left side of the brain known to be involved with processing language, and can actually wire the brain's circuits in specific ways. Linking familiar songs to new information can also help imprint information on young minds.

(2) There is also a causal link between music and spatial intelligence (the ability to perceive the world accurately and to form mental pictures of things). This kind of intelligence, by which one can visualize various elements that should go together, is critical to the sort of thinking necessary for everything from solving advanced mathematics problems to

being able to pack a book bag with everything that will be needed for the day.

(3) Recent studies show that students who study music are more successful on standardized tests such as the SAT. They also achieve higher grades in high school.

(4) Students of music learn craftsmanship as they study how details are put together painstakingly, and what constitutes good (as opposed to mediocre) work. These standards, when applied to students' own work, demand a new level of excellence and require them to stretch their inner resources.

(5) In the technical areas of music, a mistake is a mistake: the instrument is in tune or not, the notes are well played or not, the entrance is made or not. It is only by much hard work that a successful performance is possible. Through music study, students learn the value of sustained effort to achieve excellence and the concrete rewards of hard work.

(6) Music study enhances teamwork skills and discipline. In order for an orchestra to sound good, all players must work together harmoniously toward a single goal, the performance, and must commit to learning music, attending rehearsals, and practicing.

(7) Music provides children with a means of self-expression. When there is relative security in the basics of existence, the challenge is to make life meaningful and reach for a higher stage of development. Everyone needs to be in touch at some time in life with his or her core, with what he or she is and feels. Self-esteem is a by-product of this self-expression.

(8) Music study develops skills that are necessary in the workplace. It focuses on "doing" as opposed to observing, and teaches students how to perform, literally, anywhere in the world. Employers are looking for multidimensional workers with the sort of flexible and supple intellects that music education helps create as described above. In the music classroom,

students can also learn to better communicate and cooperate with one another.

(9) Music performance teaches young people to conquer fear and take risks. A little anxiety is a good thing, and something that will occur often in life. Dealing with it early and often makes it less of a problem later. Risk taking is essential if a child is to fully develop his or her potential. Music contributes to mental health and can help prevent risky behavior such as teenage drug abuse.

(10) Senior citizens benefit greatly from music-therapy intervention. Here are just a few improvements that are shown to occur:

- Better awareness and concentration.
- Enhanced interest levels and social interaction.
- Improved memory and recall.
- Happier outlook on life and higher self-esteem.
- Increased mobility and coordination.
- Diminished pain and improved recovery time.
- Reduced tension and greater relaxation.

These are just some of the benefits to learning to play a musical instrument. Think how it has affected your life, and those around you who play. Believe in music. Believe in music's benefits. You're not just in the music business; you're in the life-enhancement business.

50

Believe in Yourself

Believe in yourself, and others will be forced to believe in you.

You've seen it before. Many, many people fail to live the lives they have always wished to live. They fail to realize their ambitions and give up on their big dreams as soon as they encounter the first obstacle. One of the strongest causes for this attitude is that they do not believe in themselves.

Believing in yourself is all about being sure that you are going to do whatever you want even if others are against you. Think about it. Usually, when you decide to take a big challenge or do something that other people failed to do, you will find that everyone is putting you down.

Many times under the pressure of this criticism, some people start to doubt their own abilities and eventually give up. The few people who manage to believe in themselves and who continue moving along the path they've chosen are the ones who succeed. You need to be in this group of believers.

In almost all the cases where people give up their goals halfway through, they start their tasks being completely convinced by their ideas and are then, all of a sudden, put down by other people. Being put down is no more than convincing yourself that you are moving in the wrong direction. The problem with convincing people to believe in something is that it can easily be done regardless of which opinion is right!

Be careful when you think that other people's opinions are important. Some people think that unless everyone agrees with them, they are wrong. Not so. No one ever succeeds without being rejected.

If you don't believe in yourself, you will end up discarding your ideas, and no one will remember you. On the other hand, if you believe in yourself and continue fighting for what you want, then people may reject your ideas in the beginning, but they will be forced to believe in you in the end after seeing your success. Got it?

Hold your head up, because you have every right to. You are what you believe, and if you believe in yourself, it will show. In other words, tell yourself you are a great individual and believe in yourself, for if you don't believe in yourself, no one else will believe in you. Create your own life, and then go out and live it. If you take your eyes off your goals, all you see are obstacles.

Success breeds success. And success starts with believing in yourself!